HIGH TECHNOLOGY INDUSTRY AND INDUSTRIAL LOCATION: THE INSTRUMENTS INDUSTRY EXAMPLE

High Technology Industry and Industrial Location: the Instruments Industry Example

DR. R. P. OAKEY
University of Newcastle Upon Tyne

Gower

Published by
Gower Publishing Company Limited,
Gower House, Croft Road, Aldershot, Hampshire, England.

Reprinted 1984

British Library Cataloguing in Publication Data

Oakey, R.P.
  High technology industry and industrial location.
  1. Industries, Location of - Great Britain
  2. Technological innovations - Great Britain
  I. Title
  338.6'042'0941   HC260.D5

  ISBN 0-566-00419-4

Printed and bound in Great Britain by
Antony Rowe Ltd, Chippenham, Wiltshire

Contents

Acknowledgements

First, from many helpful members of the Geography Department at the
London School of Economics and Political Science, I must particularly
acknowledge the assistance of Prof. Michael Wise and Dr. John Martin
for their considerable advice and assistance on theoretical matters,
and specific detailed work on the preparation of the final text.
The occasional conversations and references provided by Dr. R.C. Estall
were also most welcome. For statistical and computing assistance
I respectively thank Mr. C.A. O'Muircheartaigh of the LSE Statistics
Department and Dr. S. Elgohbashi.

From experts on the Scientific and Industrial Instruments industry
I acknowledge the advice of Mr. D. Rayner of David Rayner Publications
Ltd., who gave guidance on the structure of the instruments industry
at an early stage in the research, and Mr. R. Herritage of the
Department of Industry, who made available out of print statistics.
Valuable advice and encouragement from within the Scientific and
Industrial Instruments industry was received from Mr. M.D. Carr
(Teddington Autocontrols Ltd.), Mr. S. Stone (Trumeter Company Ltd.),
and Mr. B. Treherne (Stanton Redcroft Ltd.).

I would finally like to thank my wife Dorothy for her support
throughout the duration of the research, and for typing the manuscript.

1 Background and methodological objectives

1.1. HIGH TECHNOLOGY INDUSTRY AND INDUSTRIAL GROWTH

As labour intensive industries, typified by textiles, iron and steel and motor vehicles, enter into relative or absolute decline, experts speculate on the employment potential of new high technology industries which might compensate for this otherwise depressing current industrial scene (Barron and Curnow 1979, Hines and Searle 1979). Optimists argue that new technologies based on micro-electronics will create new products (e.g. home computers, micro-chip toys), and improve the profitability of traditional forms of production through the introduction of new process technologies (e.g. robots, word processors). However, many trade unionists remain sceptical of the implications of these new technologies in industries where the application of labour saving process innovations has broad applicability (ASTMS 1978). Thus a diverse spectrum of opinion, characterised by both optimism and pessimism, offers a confused picture to the objective eye.

But much of the confusion over the industrial growth implications of high technology industries is dispelled by returning to basic manufacturing principles. If the new techniques are dichotomised at <u>plant level</u> into new product and process innovations much of the confusion is alleviated. This is not only generally applicable in considering high technology industry, but is particularly relevant to the following survey of the instruments' industry. Figure 1.1, which in a simplified manner divides both product and process technologies into 'high' and 'low' categories, provides a matrix into which individual production plants may be inserted to good effect. This model allows for the real world phenomenon in which certain plants maintain high technology

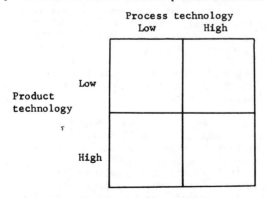

Figure 1.1 Plant level technology matrix

1

processes, but low technology products (e.g. food processing), while conversely other plants exhibit a complex product technology with a low level of process technology sophistication (e.g. scientific instruments).

Much of the muddled thinking over the employment effect of new technologies has been created by the ability of certain new machines to qualify as both product and process innovations. For example, a robot welder is a product of the plant at which it is manufactured, but a process innovation at a motor vehicle plant in which it may be set to work. Such a product, which creates or maintains jobs in the area of its manufacture, will almost certainly have greater employment impact in the various plants which purchase this innovation as a process through substantial job losses. Much the same argument applies to the manufacture and application of word processors.

Industries, and the particular plants of which they are comprised, must be evaluated individually to ascertain the employment effects of new products and processes in turn. Clearly, industries will vary considerably as to the applicability of new process techniques and the potential for product change. It might be hypothesised that industries with mature or standardised products might be generally more susceptible to new process improvements, while other industries with rapidly changing products would be, by definition, more susceptible to product change, but find the introduction of expensive process machinery difficult due to the complexity of manufacture, the small number of units produced and the constant change in specification.

This evidence from the scientific instruments' industry is particularly relevant to the argument on the effect of high technology product and process developments, since a cursory uninformed view that the instruments' industry might grow to fill gaps in employment produced by the decline of other industries will be shown to be unfounded. It will become clear that rapid product change, typical of this high technology industry, presents many problems for growth and frequently renders irrelevant the application of cost reducing process machinery.

It is clear that the impact of new high technology advances in manufacturing industry will have widely differing effects on the growth and survival of individual manufacturing sectors. Moreover, the above example of robot welders has shown that individual technological improvements will manifest spatially diverse employment effects on individual manufacturing plants depending on whether the technique is constructed or used as a process in a given location. The debate on the sectoral and spatial effects of new high technology innovation would be greatly enhanced by the introduction of more detailed evidence on the growth potential and labour requirements of industries at the centre of the high technology industrial revolution.

The following study is an attempt to introduce specific data on the scientific instruments' industry to the discussion of the employment and industrial location impacts of high technology industries on British manufacturing industry. As intimated above, this study of the instruments' industry is a rigorous test of certain rather loose arguments on the overall employment effects of high technology product and process innovations on manufacturing industry. This work also makes useful contributions to the general body of industrial location theory. Several of the preconceptions of both industrial location theory and the current debate on the impact of high technology industries are questioned by the results of this specific industrial study.

1.2. THE SCIENTIFIC AND INDUSTRIAL INSTRUMENTS INDUSTRY

The study of a single sector or branch of industry has a long and distinguished history within industrial location research (Hoover 1937, Cotterill 1950, Hague and Newman 1952, Taylor 1971, North 1974). Hence an approach to the improvement of industrial geographical knowledge through the study of a particular sector of industry requires no justification. However, the particular choice of the Scientific and Industrial Instruments and Systems Industry (Minimum List Heading 354) as the subject for this research was made for two main reasons.

First, the industry is of particular interest because, although it possesses characteristics of contemporary significance to industrial geography, it has received scant attention from researchers. Three relevant studies exist from USA sources (Spiegelman 1964, Farness 1968, Gibson 1970) which have dealt with the instruments industry in the USA to varying extents but no comprehensive work has been produced on the British industry. Second, as argued above, evidence from a study of this high technology industry is particularly relevant to the current debate on the growth potential of high technology industries.

Indeed, the instruments industry in the post war period has grown in both size and importance due to the rapid increase in the automation of industrial process machinery and the subsequent demand for control instrumentation. These industrial control instruments now form a large part of total MLH 354 production by value of output (evident in the structural section to follow). In the role of supplier of key products which form component parts of automated machinery made by firms in other industrial sectors, MLH 354 exercises technological influence in many other industries.

1.3. METHODOLOGICAL OBJECTIVES

It is accepted that the characteristics of MLH 354 are highly specialised in nature and that factors of locational importance to instrument production cannot be necessarily asserted as applicable to an explanation of the general location of industry. However, important new light is thrown by this study on industries displaying high technology, high value added and labour oriented characteristics.

The general hypothesis of this study asserts that the particular high technology nature of MLH 354 production is central to any attempt to define the criteria which affect the location of both new and established firms within the industry. This general assertion should be no surprise, since it has been a constant feature of sectoral studies of industry that changes in technology and methods of production frequently produce radical effects on the geographical distribution of the industries studied (Warren 1969, Chapman 1973).

3

In the MLH 354 instance it was expected that the high technology nature of MLH 354 production could cause individual location factors to be relevant or irrelevant to the location of instrument industry production. For example, the generally complex products of the industry might reduce the locational importance of local linkages due to the frequently large number and exacting specification of components required by MLH 354 plants. It was considered unlikely that such complex inputs would be available from within the local industrial environment. But, the same complex product specifications might render labour significant due to the importance of skilled labour inputs to the production process.

However, it was decided that an in depth study of all the location factors relevant to MLH 354 production was required. By adopting this broad approach, not only the factors of importance to MLH 354 location would be identified, but location factors of low locational importance would also be examined and eliminated. By testing all potential location influencing factors regardless of preconceptions, and approaching their importance to MLH 354 with no methodological bias, a secure level of objectivity has been aimed for. The following chapters attempt to build a comprehensive picture of the locational environment of the Scientific and Industrial Instruments and Systems industry.

2 The survey design

2.1. DATA GATHERING

Many practical advantages attach to a study of MLH 354 in Britain. First, the industry is relatively small in absolute size (i.e. 1,096 establishments in 1972). Hence, the general technological homogeneity of the industry and the relatively small number of establishments ensured that the subsequent study sample was a reasonable proportion of the total industry, providing good statistical significance for the survey results. Secondly, the 'clean' nature of MLH 354 production, and the generally high levels of education exhibited by instrument firm executives were considered to create a favourable environment for the completion of an interview questionnaire survey.

The topic of study and the nature of the approach having been established, the problems of empirical data gathering became readily apparent. There are two main approaches used by academic researchers to the obtaining of data on industrial location. First, previously collected government statistics may provide a basis for analysis. However, such data have the disadvantage of being collected to satisfy government objectives and are, in many respects, not applicable to the study to which they are adapted. But in any case, in the context of the present study, no suitable data were available on MLH 354.

The second method of data gathering, chosen for this study, is the development of an industrial survey in which actual decision makers within the industry concerned are interviewed to gain empirical information. This method possesses the advantage of allowing the researcher to construct questions which isolate precisely the topics deemed relevant to the study.

2.2. THE QUESTIONNAIRE

There are two main methods of conducting a questionnaire survey. These are either by dispatching a postal questionnaire to respondents or by adopting a personal interview approach. Townroe (1971) argues strongly that, if possible, the personal interview method of enquiry should be adopted since it offers major methodological advantages. Indeed, the only clear advantage of a postal questionnaire is the much lower unit cost of completion, allowing a larger survey. However, for industrial studies of the type carried out here, the interview method offers the invaluable facility of actually getting to grips with the particular industry studied, thus gaining a visual and mental impression of the physical realities of the study area which can never be gained from statistical tables or postal questionnaire forms.

Further, the interview method allows the interviewer to elaborate on any particular question that might cause difficulty. Experience gained from the interview survey of this study would suggest that this facility is a major advantage. For although it must be accepted that the bulk of all government and academic industrial inquiry must be based on the results of questionnaires of various types, the method is not without important drawbacks. Central to an understanding of questionnaire results is the need to accept the reality that responses are a form of subjective evaluation and are not necessarily objective facts. A questionnaire seeking a respondent's view on a particular point may gain a precise response. However, the only concrete fact that may be positively deduced is that the question was answered. It does not follow, even if the questions were fully understood, that the response is an objective fact.

Frequently the interviewer may feel that the question has not been answered objectively, but it is not the task of the interviewer to bias responses by arguing with an interviewee over the accuracy of certain replies. Provided the question has been fully understood (and again it may be stated that the ability to ascertain this is the major advantage of the personal interview method), the answer must be accepted as fact. Indeed, the response is fact in the sense that it represents a subjective appraisal of a particular topic. Moreover, studies of industrial location decision making have shown that important plant location decisions are frequently taken on the basis of very poor information (Cameron and Clark 1966, Townroe 1971,1973). Hence, wildly inaccurate evaluations of location criteria may be important if they serve as a basis for decision making within the industrial firm.

Even responses to precise quantitative questions, for example the number of workers employed, occasionally met with highly subjective responses. Indeed, it was interesting to note that on the few occasions that the questionnaire was jointly answered by two executives the level of disagreement, even on very simple questions, was quite striking. Thus it is not surprising that questions on environmental quality, or the quality of local skilled labour, might produce wide differences in responses from firms in the same local area. In the light of these observations, the work produced by Stafford (1974) in which content analysis is used in order to delve more deeply into the motivations behind response patterns is only of small additional value, since it does not deal with the variability in the accuracy of response.

The major source of inaccuracy in questionnaire surveys undoubtedly stems from this variable accuracy of replies, and not from the form of questionnaire design. However, this does not negate the need for the utmost rigour in questionnaire design to eliminate any ambiguities and to ensure that accurate and unambiguous information is obtained. Moreover, in the context of the whole study, the minority of seriously questionable responses should be rendered insignificant through aggregation, and accurate general impressions should emerge.

The questionnaire of the present study was designed to incorporate all location factors considered to be of importance, or possible importance, to MLH 354. An introductory section which established the basic characteristics of the individual plant determined the 'type code'. This type code was developed in order to ensure that individual plants were not asked irrelevant questions. For example, it would be pointless to question a plant which had been established in a location for many years on the problems of relocation. Hence four type codes were devised in order to define the major categories of industrial plant encountered in this study. These were:

    A. Single plant (established).
    B. Single plant (new location).
    C. Multi plant (established).
    D. Multi plant (new location).

Questions were precoded with the relevant letter and, once an individual plant had been coded, only questions which were preceded by the plant's individual code letter were used. Thus a question coded ABCD would be put to all sample plants and questions coded CD would only apply to multi plant establishments (typically these questions would be concerned with the organisational structure of the group to which the individual plant belonged). This system of coding proved to be highly efficient and saved valuable time during interview sessions. Sections on organisation, information, materials, transport, markets, labour and behaviour followed the introductory section of the questionnaire. The questionnaire was then tested on a pilot sample of six plants in order to assess the performance of each individual question and to gauge the average length of interview.

It was estimated that one hour should be the optimum length of time devoted to each interview, balancing the desire for maximum information with the dangers of a low response rate which might result from potential interviewees being daunted by the prospect of a long and involved cross-examination. It was discovered that the 110 questions could be covered, on average, within one hour. Further, although all the questions appeared to function well, it was decided to produce an explanatory leaflet which was given to respondents at the beginning of interviews as a means of defining certain parameters used during the interview.

2.3. THE CHOICE OF SAMPLE

It was clearly not economically or temporally feasible to conduct interviews at all the 1,096 establishments classified to MLH 354. Thus some form of sample was obviously indicated. It was decided to aim for a survey sample of 100 plants as this number would represent approximately ten per cent of the total number of establishments classified to MLH 354. A ten per cent sample of the total population is an acceptable proportion and statistically strengthens the results of the present survey.

In a sense, it would have been ideal to sample plants on a national basis to ensure a representation of establishments from all the planning regions of Britain. However, three major

7

difficulties decreased the attractiveness of this strategy. First, as will be noted from Table 2.1., the distribution of MLH 354 employment is highly concentrated, and the selection of plants on a national planning region basis would not have reflected the distribution of MLH 354 production. Second, the disaggregation of the desired 100 plant main sample into ten planning region sub-groups would have rendered any sub-regional analysis statistically impossible. But the third and overpowering argument against a national sample was the constraint of finance. The cost of a national survey, on either a regionally stratified or a random basis (given that the personal interview method was considered essential) would have been economically crippling.

Table 2.1.
Regional distribution of MLH 354 employment
(1971)

Standard planning region	Employees (000's)	Percentage of U.K. MLH 354 employment
North	2.3	1.9
Yorks and Humberside	3.2	2.6
East Midlands	3.4	2.8
East Anglia	4.2	3.5
South East	62.9	52.5
South West	7.7	6.4
West Midlands	5.0	4.2
North West	18.8	15.7
Wales	1.9	1.5
Scotland	10.3	8.7

As a result of these considerations, it was decided to conduct the survey in the North West and South East planning regions. It will be noted from Table 2.1. that these regions virtually choose themselves, as the two most important regions for the employment of MLH 354 labour. It might be anticipated that parts of the North West planning region would suffer from the problems of industrial dereliction and a poor general environment, contrasting with the generally cleaner industrial environment of the South East. In particular, it was expected that, as noted by Buswell and Lewis (1970), skilled technical and administrative staff might display positive preferences for general environmental quality which could disadvantage the North West planning region.

Having chosen the study regions, the actual sampling procedure followed. The bane of all industrial field studies is the dearth of names and addresses when empirical work is operationalised. Because of existing laws on the disclosure of privileged information most government statistics are not disaggregated to the level of the individual plant. However, it was a requirement of this study that plants included in the sample frame were predominantly involved in MLH 354 production (i.e. over 50 per cent of total output by value).

Fortunately, it was possible to obtain two reliable directories from which the sampling was conducted. These directories were of enhanced value because they classified establishments accurately to MLH 354. The first source was the government publication 'The directory of businesses: instrument engineering; electrical engineering' (1968). Unfortunately this directory did not include plants employing less than 25 workers. A small percentage of addresses included in the sample were found to have been vacated by the plants concerned and were subsequently replaced. But the majority of addresses were used in the survey and, most importantly, all indicated establishments classified to MLH 354. The second data source was the 'United Kingdom instrument manufacturers' directory (Rayner 1974). This was an excellent source of data, as it included establishments employing less than 25 workers and also gave the number of workers employed in each plant.

Establishments included from the government directory were initially contacted by means of a letter/form which was returned in the majority of cases, giving details of the number of workers employed. As a result, for the South East, a sample frame of 367 plants was derived for which employment sizes were known, obtained from either the United Kingdom instrument manufacturers directory or the above mentioned employment size survey. These plants were then sampled on a stratified basis, according to size, using random number tables. This ensured that the final South East study sample of 100 plants accurately reflected the sampling frame.

A group of 50 establishments from the North West planning region was added to the South East plants. It was intended to use these 150 establishments as a basis for initial enquiries. This procedure anticipated that a 33 per cent wastage would result from factory closures and interview refusals, leaving the desired final sample of approximately 100 plants, 33 establishments in the small North West planning region and 66 plants from the South East. The 50 plants in the North West planning region were not a stratified sample of North West plants but represented the total number of establishments available from directory sources. The final group of plants interviewed from the two planning regions consisted of 102 plants (i.e. 66 establishments from the South East and 36 establishments in the North West). If factory closures are excluded, and non-response is confined to actual interview refusals, the response rate was 82.9 per cent.

2.4. METHODS OF ANALYSIS

The main survey questionnaire comprised 110 questions, many of which had up to nine parts. Clearly, the possible permutations of response patterns produced by the 102 plants in the survey were immense. Hence, the use of a computer programme was indicated in order to sort the large amount of information generated from the survey into meaningful groupings, suitable for detailed analysis. Because of the individual nature of the quesionnaire design, it was decided that a specially constructed computer programme was needed to sort the questionnaire data. A Fortran 4 computer programme was therefore devised to organise the data in the form required. In particular, codes were designed to record any changes from city centre to the planning region boundary in the response patterns of firms. These codes corresponded to sectors based on the four

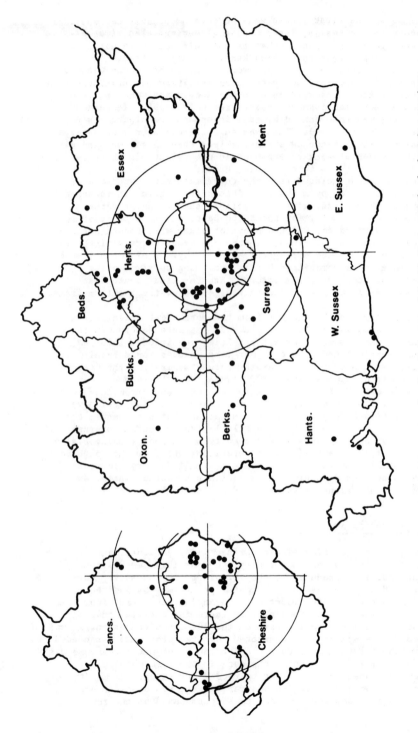

Figure 2.1 The study sample distribution in the North West and South East standard planning regions (circles drawn at 15 mile intervals)

points of the compass, and centred on the major urban centres within the two planning regions (i.e. London and Manchester). Two circles were then added, centred on the same urban focus at 15 mile intervals, thus creating 12 coded sectors (Figure 2.1).

Once the general sorting of the data had been completed, the data were then easily subjected to specific statistical analysis. Various possible forms of aggregate analysis were considered (e.g. multiple regression, principal components analysis), but it was decided that such methods imposed constraints on methodology and the manner in which the data are analysed, frequently producing aggregate results which fail to isolate important variables existant in a detailed study of this type. Instead cross tabulations arising from computer analysis were tested for statistical significance throughout this study by means of chi square tests. In instances where two sets of ordinal scale variables occur, correlations were performed. However, in the main, chi square tests predominate, since a questionnaire, by its nature of frequently demanding yes/no responses to questions, is not particularly suitable for forms of analysis which require two sets of ordinal variables.

This study adopts the positive approach of testing specific hypotheses which were suggested either by the general literature on industrial location or by impressions gained during the months of fieldwork spent in MLH 354 establishments. The following analysis presents a consideration of the MLH 354 survey results in eight major empirical chapters under the following headings:

Structure	Linkages
Organisation	Labour
Information	Behaviour
Transport	New location and relocation

The ordering of the sections has been devised to produce a logical flow, grouping organisation with information, and transport with linkages. Labour, behaviour and new location and relocation are considered last since these sectors were discovered to include the most significant location influencing results. In the final chapters the results will be drawn together for concluding analysis in the light of existing literature on industrial location theory in general and high technology industry in particular.

3 Structure

3.1. INTRODUCTION

This short section has been included as a means of introducing the general structural characteristics of the scientific and industrial instruments and systems industry, through a synopsis of available government statistics. A perspective on the data produced by the following empirical chapters is created by including such a consideration at this point, allowing a firmer understanding of the activities which constitute MLH 354 production.

MLH 354 is an industrial sector that is continuously undergoing improvements in the technology of its products. This rapidly changing technology presents problems of classification since certain instruments, through improvements in technological specification, may require re-classification under a different product heading within MLH 354. A historical example of this problem is the technological change from clockwork and mechanical control to electronic circuits and relays. Further, new instruments, resulting from completely new forms of high technology, regularly enter the sector and need to be classified either under an existing product heading, or under a completely new heading of its own. The case of ultra-sonic instruments is an example of a new technological type of instrument that necessitated a new product heading.

The major change in structural emphasis that has occured within the past 25 years has been the rapid growth in the manufacture of industrial control instruments as a result of the extension of mechanisation in manufacturing industry. The traditional view of the instruments industry has been of skilled craftsmen making microscopes, barometers, balances and surveying equipment. However, this chapter will confirm that it is industrial measuring and control instruments that account for the major share of MLH 354 sales today.

It was partly as a response to the major growth in the manufacture of industrial control instruments, which did not fit easily into the previous 1963 'Scientific, surgical and photographic instruments (part 53)' Minimum List Heading, that the Business Statistics Office made major changes to the Standard Industrial Classification in 1968. The new 1968 Minimum List Heading 354 was a real improvement, rendering the instruments industry Minimum List Heading more technologically homogeneous. Major exclusions were most photographic instruments and spectacles.

The exclusion of these product types made the classification more meaningful from the viewpoint of technological homogeneity but, due to their significant financial contribution to the value of total sales in the 1963 'Scientific, surgical and photographic instruments' sector, detailed statistical comparisons between 1963 and 1968 are not possible. Further, the inclusion of instruments for measuring and testing electronic magnitudes, instruments for physical and chemical analysis, nucleonic instruments, gas and electricity meters, parking meters and taxi meters, improved the 1968 classification. But as with the exclusions, these inclusions render any statistical comparison between the 1963 and 1968 Minimum List Headings completely meaningless. However, for certain limited aggregated information 1963 data are expressed in the form of the 1968 classification.

Hence, the bulk of available time series data on the instruments industry begins in 1968. In some respects it is disappointing, but conversely, the advantage of technological homogeneity facilitated by the 1968 re-classification has helped this study in many other respects. The inclusion of cameras and spectacles under an instruments sector heading would have introduced variables peculiar to these types of production that were not characteristic of true instrument industry production.

The data given below are taken from the annual reports on the Census of Production 1968 to 1972, and the Business Monitor Quarterly Statistics 1972 to 1975. The 1968 Census of Production includes a limited amount of re-classified data from the 1963 Census of Production. From mid-1971 the Business Statistics Office has produced a quarterly breakdown of MLH 354 output at the level of product type, giving a useful insight into the shares that each product and product group hold within MLH 354 total production. Statistics on MLH 354 exports are also included but are presented in the chapter on linkages, under a consideration of exports. The analysis begins with an examination of the size characteristics of MLH 354 establishments.

3.2. SIZE OF PLANT AND OUTPUT

The data in Table 3.1. indicate the absolute size of MLH 354 between 1963 and 1972. The most significant information in this table is the relatively small number of firms classified to the industry, numbering 970 enterprises and 1,096 establishments in 1972. It is of further interest to observe that while the number of establishments has decreased slightly between 1968 and 1972, both the number of enterprises and net output have consistently increased.

A logical explanation for the increased numbers of enterprises, while establishments have decreased in numbers, is that multi plant firms are rationalising their organisational structure and reducing the number of plants within their group. This would account for the reduction in the number of establishments. Conversely, the entry of small firms would explain the increase in the number of enterprises.

It should be remembered that small firms are often single plant organisations and thus an establishment, no matter how small, equates with an enterprise. Further, for large organisations, the death of one enterprise can mean the subsequent closure of several establishments. Clearly, there is a death rate of enterprises throughout the firm size ranges, but the replacement rate must be higher among the smaller firms than for large enterprises.

Table 3.1
Scientific and industrial instruments and systems (MLH 354)

Year	Number of enterprises	Number of establishments	Average output per establishment (£)	Net output (£)
1963	750	930	143,334	133,301,000
1968	945	1,160	190,445	220,982,000
1970	940	1,024	236,160	241,828,000
1972	970	1,096	241,655	264,854,000

Source: Census of Production

It would have been interesting to analyse the data in Table 3.2 in terms of size categories to ascertain if the above assertions could be proven. However, this was not possible since in the Census of Production figures for enterprises, the individual size category sub-totals add up to a figure that is greater than the grand total. This discrepancy is caused by an enterprise appearing in more than one size category. But this does not effect the accuracy of the grand totals in Table 3.2.

The overall growth in numbers of plants within the 1-99 employee size category is most marked. However, the importance of small establishments to MLH 354 should not be exaggerated. For example, in 1972 plants in the 1-99 employees size categories numbered 910 establishments (83 per cent of MLH 354 total) and produced a net output to the value of £42,272,000. But in the over 1,000 employee category, 22 establishments (2 per cent of the MLH 354 total) produced a net output of £96,316,000. Clearly, neither absolute numbers of plants nor output will provide a universal measure of importance to MLH 354. Both measures may be useful in specific analytical operations, depending upon the task undertaken.

A further point worthy of brief consideration here is the fact that output has increased while the number of establishments producing goods has decreased. A degree of efficiency resulting from rationalisation might explain a proportion of this greater average output per establishment. Certainly, the total number of employees classified to the industry fell by 10,501 workers between 1968 and 1972. However, inflation must explain some of the apparent increase in sales.

3.3. PLANT SIZE AND OUTPUT PER HEAD

The most striking statistic to emerge from the tables presented here involves the average ouput per employee shown by MLH 354 establishments. Table 3.2 indicates that for 1970 and 1972

14

Table 3.2
Analysis of MLH 354 establishments by size

	Estab.	*Enter.	Empl.	(£000's) Net output	(£) Net output per head
			1968		
1-99	863	832	17,859	21,561	3,616
100-199	94	73	13,319	23,704	1,780
200-499	81	51	24,844	45,072	1,814
500-749	20	14	12,540	25,322	2,019
750-999	14	13	12,398	23,802	1,920
1,000+over	24	20	40,265	70,005	1,739
Total**	1,160	945	121,498	220,982	1,819
			1970		
1-99	829	824	16,344	35,367	2,143
100-199	65	62	8,935	22,763	2,540
200-499	71	66	21,909	43,722	1,996
500-749	24	20	16,012	33,780	2,110
750-999	12	10	11,302	19,757	1,748
1,000+over	23	21	48,309	86,440	1,789
Total	1,024	940	122,811	241,829	1,966
			1972		
1-99	910	884	16,514	42,272	2,421
100-199	68	64	10,552	26,638	2,517
200-499	68	67	20,762	52,053	2,507
500-749	19	14	11,621	32,280	2,778
750-999	9	9	7,872	16,905	2,147
1,000+over	22	19	43,671	96,316	2,205
Total	1,096	970	110,992	266,464	2,379

* The sum of the figures in the size groups exceeds the total for the industry because certain enterprises made returns for establishments in more than one size group.

** Totals include 64 establishments (and their statistics) not classified by size.

(dates for which figures are directly comparable), establishments
in the 1-99 employees group averaged £2,143 per head and £2,421
per head respectively. But in the 750-999 and over 1,000 workers
size groups for these years the output per head was:

	1970
750-999	£1,748
Over 1,000	£1,789

	1972
750-999	£2,147
Over 1,000	£2,205

These figures clearly show that for both 1970 and 1972, small
establishments boasted a better output per head than the larger
firms within MLH 354. These data are surprising in that they
conflict with the generally held notion that large establishments,
through reductions in unit costs resulting from more mechanised
production methods, are able to reap economies of scale and
obtain a higher output per head. Clearly, this trend is not
evident within MLH 354. Indeed, the figures indirectly suggest
that mass production process technologies may be difficult to
operationalise in MLH 354 production plants, and indeed that
small establishments are more efficient than their larger
MLH 354 competitors.

   Throughout the following chapters, the individuality and technical
complexity of MLH 354 products will be a recurrent theme. It will
be frequently noted that high technology and specialised markets
(with products often being made to customers' specifications) have
a profound effect upon the location of MLH 354. Indeed, the
following survey results on the importance of shopfloor labour
will support the assertion that large MLH 354 firms are not able to
make the economies of scale through mechanisation which are
evident in other forms of industrial production.

3.4. MLH 354 PRODUCTS

Here the objective is to indicate the types of products produced
within MLH 354. Table 3.3. lists both the value of sales and the
proportion of total MLH 354 sales for each product category. It
is clear that there has been little change in the relative product
shares over the period 1972 to 1975. As previously stated, process
measuring and control instruments are the largest
group of products, accounting for 42.9 per cent of total sales
within MLH 354 in 1975. This product group is the backbone of
MLH 354 output, increasing its sales by £98,213,000 between 1972
and 1975.

   The remaining 57.1 per cent of MLH 354 production is spread
more evenly among the remaining twelve product groups. Electrical
measuring and control instruments is the second largest with 12.2 per
cent of total sales in 1975. The optical instruments and appliances
group is a poor third in importance with 7 per cent of 1975 sales.
The sales of the remaining nine product groups range from less than
one per cent of total sales to the 6.9 per cent achieved by

Table 3.3
Major product headings of MLH 354 giving sales by value (000's)
and proportion of total sales: 1972 to 1975

	1972		1973		1974		1975	
	£	%	£	%	£	%	£	%
Optical instruments and appliances	26,695	7.3	31,272	7.7	31,395	6.6	40,953	7.0
Surveying, hydrographic navigational, meteorological and geophysical instruments (non-optical except magnetic compasses and gyroscopes)	8,643	2.4	9,533	2.3	12,037	2.5	13,713	2.4
Instruments for engineering metrology	5,378	1.5	6,506	1.6	9,072	1.9	9,530	1.6
Instruments, apparatus or models for educational or exhibition purposes	3,360	0.9	3,752	0.9	4,059	0.8	5,087	0.9
Instruments, apparatus for testing physical and mechanical properties of materials and for non-destructive testing of homogeneity (excluding ultra-sonic equipment)	5,328	1.5	6,973	1.7	9,333	2.0	10,667	1.8
Process measuring and control instruments and systems	152,770	41.6	167,587	41.1	193,281	40.6	250,982	42.9
Analytical instruments	20,515	5.6	25,941	6.4	33,985	7.1	40,703	6.9
Liquid, gas and electricity supply meters and pre-paid meters	26,874	7.3	26,884	6.6	31,161	6.6	39,724	6.8

continued ..

17

Table 3.3 (continued)

	1972		1973		1974		1975	
	£	%	£	%	£	%	£	%
Counting and velocity measuring instruments	19,360	5.3	18,037	4.4	21,226	4.5	23,855	4.1
Electrical measuring, testing and controlling instruments and apparatus	44,737	12.2	53,203	13.0	60,709	12.8	71,190	12.2
Ultra-sonic instruments and equipment	1,046	0.3	1,507	0.4	2,223	0.5	2,434	0.4
Scientific laboratory instruments and apparatus not elsewhere specified	8,587	2.3	6,797	1.7	8,456	1.8	8,559	1.5
Other scientific and industrial instruments not elsewhere specified	14,704	4.0	16,243	4.0	18,291	3.8	22,866	3.9
TOTALS*	367,133	92.2	408,165	91.8	475,629	91.6	584,534	92.4

* Percentages do not add up to 100 per cent due to the exclusion of
parts and accessories and unclassified work done. The totals
of sales, by value, are greater than those shown in Table 3.1
as they do not include costs of materials and services
purchased and transport

analytical instruments. Optical instruments and appliances,
although given a separate sub-section within MLH 354 (i.e. 354/1)
accounts for a mere 7 per cent of MLH 354 total sales. The
remaining 12 product groups together provide 93 per cent of MLH 354
total sales, but are grouped together in the second sub-section
(i.e. 354/2).

3.5. CONCLUSION

In this brief review of government statistics on MLH 354 the
relatively small absolute size of the industry is apparent. The
share that each product group holds within MLH 354 has also been
indicated. The most impressive information to be extracted from
the tables concerns small establishments, especially in the

1-99 size group. This group indicated an overall growth in plant
numbers, outstripping all other plant size categories. To an
extent this growth would be anticipated in the smallest size groups,
but the figures on output per head are most surprising. The high
output per head among small establishments may help to explain some
of their success. However, the high output per head of small
establishments in comparison with large plants must largely
stem from the inability of large firms to introduce a standardised
mass production process technology. The inability of MLH 354
production units to reduce production costs, through the
introduction of economies of scale, is central to an understanding
of MLH 354 production, and is of wider significance to a consideration
of the employment potential of high technology industries. This
theme will re-occur throughout this study and in the concluding
chapter.

4 Organisation

4.1. INTRODUCTION

There is ample evidence to substantiate the important role played
by multi plant industrial firms in determining the location of
modern manufacturing industry (Parsons 1972, Rees 1972, 1974,
Leigh and North 1978, Goddard and Smith 1978, Smith 1979). This
chapter of the study is specifically concerned with the manner
in which the organisation of MLH 354 production influences the
location of the instruments industry. As is the case throughout
this work, the results from this study of MLH 354 will be
related to relevant literature whenever appropriate. For, as
McNee (1974) has argued, empirical case studies are required in
order to test the mass of literature that progressively appears
pertaining to industrial organisations, much of it unsubstantiated.

It has been acknowledged that valuable contributions have been
made to the literature on the spatial complexity of the multi
plant industrial organisation and its effect upon the geographical
distribution of industry. However, although such contributions are
of great value in this important field of research, it should not
be assumed that because multi plant firms have, by definition,
a complex spatial organisational structure, then single plant
firms are conversely simple in the plant level aspects of
organisation. The organisation of these single plant firms,
while obviously not spatial, may be considerably more complex
than a branch factory of a multi plant organisation, when
compared at plant level. For the single plant firm, although
characterised by low levels of turnover and employment, has
all the operations of the firm under one roof.

With regard to Figure 4.1, it should be noted that while
Figure 4.1.B can be presented as a reasonable generalisation of
the organisational structure of any single plant firm, the degree
of autonomy that any individual branch plant may display cannot
be standardised in the same way. Consequently, it should be
stressed that Figure 4.1.A is a hypothetically extreme model
of a branch plant experiencing a high degree of central control.
The work of certain writers would suggest that, for specific
sectors of industry, the Figure 4.1.A model is applicable
(Luttrell 1962, Townroe 1971). However, it remains for this
chapter to ascertain the degree of autonomy displayed by branch
plants within MLH 354.

As can be seen from Figure 4.2, the degree of control that
each individual sample establishment can exercise may be generally
depicted in simple terms. Single plant firms and headquarter
factories of multi plant organisations within the survey sample
are similar in that they both exhibit total control over their

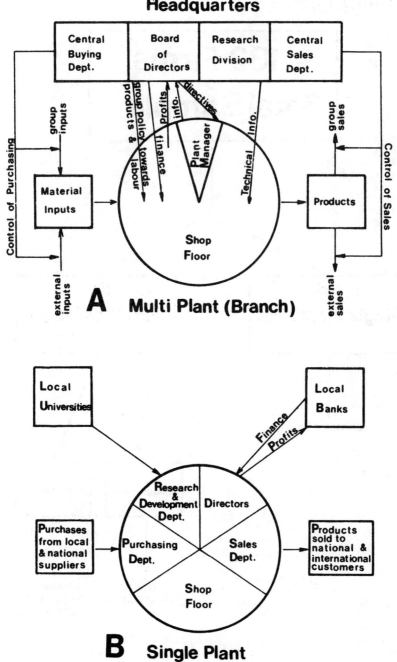

Figure 4.1   Multi plant and single plant organisational differences

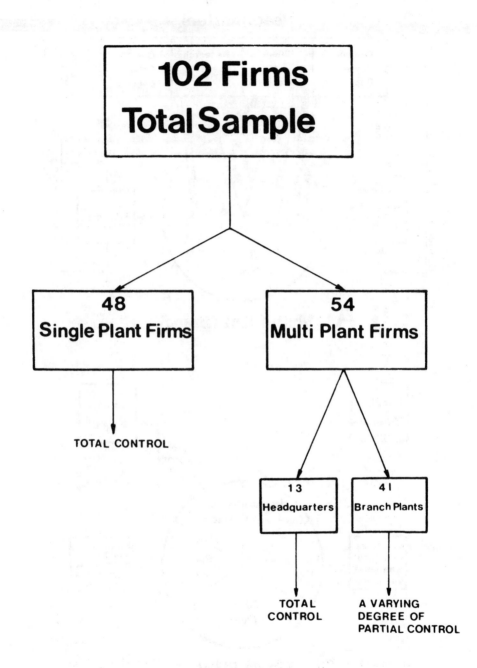

Figure 4.2 Degree of control in survey firms

own premises. Such establishments comprise 61 plants in the total
sample (59.8 per cent). The 41 remaining plants are, to a varying
extent, dependent upon a separate headquarters for a portion of their
decision making, the importance of which varies with the establishment
concerned.

4.2. PURCHASING FREEDOM IN BRANCH PLANTS

Here consideration must necessarily be given to the 41 branch
factories within the sample. The 48 single plant independent firms
and 13 headquarters factories have, by definition, total organisational
freedom.

A specific question inquiring whether freedom to purchase or
contract was total, permissible for some items, or only possible
after consulting headquarters, was put to senior esecutives in
the 41 branch plants. In a general comparison with the work of
Luttrell (1962) and Townroe (1971) the results expressed in
Table 4.1 display a marked tendency towards a high degree of
internal control by MLH 354 branch plants. At a more specific

Table 4.1
Freedom to purchase or contract

	Number	Percentage
Total freedom	36	87.8
Permissible for some items	4	9.8
Only permissible after contacting headquarters	1	2.4
Total	41	100.0

level, it is of interest to encorporate data on linkages. By
adopting a single independent firm/branch plant comparison, and
analysing only establishments who derived over 50 per cent of their
material inputs locally, it is clear that branch plants make a
marginally greater use of local material suppliers than do single
plant independent firms (Table 4.2). Further, it is clear that this

Table 4.2
Comparison of single plant and branch plant purchases

	Single plant		Branch plant	
	N	%	N	%
Proportion of material inputs purchased locally:				
50-74%	8	30.8	12	46.2
75-100%	4	15.4	2	7.7
Total	12	46.2	14	53.9

larger dependence of branch plant firms on local material supplies
is not a result of local intra-group supply relationships. The
passage of materials from other plants of the group, both locally
and nationally, were insignificant. Questions gauged the significance

of local material supplies from other plant members (for full treatment
see Chapter 7). It was considered that if material supplies were to
be relevant at all, they would be more prevalent among closely
juxtapositioned plants of the same organisation.

Only 14 of the 32 multi plant establishments with local group members
acknowledged receipts of group material supplies, and of these plants,
12 received less than 25 per cent of their total material inputs from
other local plants of their group (most considerably less). One
plant received between 25-49 per cent and one plant received between
50-74 per cent. These results suggest very low material supply
interaction among multi plant establishments in the survey sample.

The results from this analysis of organisational independence
towards purchasing among MLH 354 branch plants indicate a high general
level of internal control.

4.3. ORGANISATIONAL ENTERPRISE TOWARDS INFORMATION

Here an attempt is made to test the effort made by plant executives
in their search of the industrial environment for new technical
and administrative information. Chapter 5, on the impact of
information on location, will offer a more comprehensive treatment
of this subject. In the present context, emphasis will be placed
upon the organisational aspects of information gathering which
involve a variability of choice on the part of the entrepreneur
involved. Since these choices are a reflection of an establishment's
organisational strategy, they will vary with the needs and goals
perceived by senior executives.

It was considered that size, used in conjunction with the multi
plant/single plant dichotomy might be a useful determinant of the
variability in effort and attitudes in sample plants. Dicken
(1971, p432) asserts that 'Under present economic and technological
conditions, large organisations are the most active innovators
investing a greater proportion of their resources in research and
development'. While it is beyond the scope of this present study
to examine the research and development effort of all the plants
within a large corporation, it is possible to compare the R & D ·
performance of multi plants with that of independent single plant
firms in this study. Since multi plant establishments have been
shown to be generally larger than their single plant independent
counterparts, it might be initially hypothesised that they could,
due to economies of scale, invest a greater proportion of their
resources to R & D. (See Table 4.5 for plant size/status relationship).

Questions were designed to gauge the individual plant's approach
to information gathering. An initial enquiry asked if the factory
belonged to any trade or industrial associations. The results of
this question indicate that larger plants within the sample tended
to be members of at least one association or official body, while
small plants did not. This trend is statistically supported
by the chi square test, significant at the $p = 0.001$ per cent level
(Table 4.3). However, the results in this table must be qualified by the
observation that, during interviews, very little enthusiasm was

generally shown by plant executives for these official representative bodies. Frequently enquiries were made by the interviewees to ascertain if their plant was affiliated to any trade or industrial association before the question could be answered. This suggests that official associations are not a great source of regular information, and consequently might explain why small plants with restricted amounts of finance are less willing to join an association that may produce a poor return on time and money invested.

Table 4.3
Membership of trade or industrial associations

Plant size (number of employees)	Yes		No	
	N	%*	N	%*
1-19	1	11.1	8	88.9
20-49	11	35.5	20	64.5
50-99	15	68.2	7	31.8
100-199	10	83.3	2	16.7
200-499	13	81.3	3	18.7
500-999	8	88.9	1	11.1
1000+over	3	100.0	0	0.0
Total	61	59.8	41	40.2

chi square = 27.8   p = 0.001

* Proportion of total respondents in any given plant size category

A stronger measure of plant enterprise towards the organisation of information is the number of workers employed in research and development. This is a more reliable measure of actual investment of resources in the constant search for technical information which leads to more sophisticated and competitive products. Indeed, in an industry where technical specification and innovation are as important as price, the constant need to update products should be reflected in the number of workers involved in the development of new products.

However, the organisation of manpower between direct and indirect labour can be an acute problem for the small independent firm. For example, in an establishment of less than 20 employees, an extra man employed in research and development constitutes one less worker who could be producing saleable goods. Small firm executives are only too well aware of this problem and hence, the number of workers employed in research and development are a clear reflection of a firm's attitude towards the organisation of manpower resources.

The first test compared the number of workers in research and development with the organisational status of survey plants (Table 4.4). This table shows, in accordance with a large plant/high investment in research and development hypothesis, a large bias in favour of multi plant firms (a chi square test was significant at the p = 0.001 level). This is almost certainly due to the fact that multi plant establishments are also generally the largest (Table 4.5). To further support this assertion, a correlation was performed upon the two sets of ordinal data, total number or workers (independent variable) and number of workers employed in research and development

25

(dependent variable). A correlation coefficient of r = 0.7042 was obtained, confirming the strong level of association between these two sets of variables.

Table 4.4
Number of workers in research and development by organisational status

Number of research workers	Single plant		Multi plant	
	N	%*	N	%*
1-4	31	65.9	16	34.1
5-9	11	50.0	11	50.0
10-19	3	42.9	4	57.1
20-29	2	22.2	7	77.8
30-49	1	16.7	5	83.3
50-99	-	-	7	100.0
100+over	-	-	4	100.0
Total	48	47.1	54	52.9

chi square = 17.7   p = 0.001
* Proportion of total respondents in any given plant size category

Table 4.5
Plant size by organisational status

Plant size (number of employees)	Single plant		Multi plant	
	N	%*	N	%*
1-19	8	88.9	1	11.1
20-49	23	74.2	8	25.8
50-99	9	40.9	13	59.1
100-199	5	41.7	7	58.3
200-499	3	18.7	13	81.3
500-999	-	-	9	100.0
1,000+over	-	-	3	100.0
Total	48	47.1	54	52.9

chi square = 30.8   p = 0.001
* Proportion of total respondents in any given plant size category

However, a more relevant analysis was performed in which the previous two tests were re-employed, but with the dependent variable altered from number of workers in research and development to the number of workers in research and development expressed as a proportion of the total workforce. From these two further tests, the chi square test yielded no significance at the p = 0.05 level (Table 4.6) and a weak correlation coefficient value of r = 0.1386 was achieved. The most significant generalisation that may be drawn from the above tests, certainly in terms of MLH 354, is that while multi plant establishments almost certainly contribute a larger proportion of resources to MLH 354's total research and development budget, they do not invest a greater proportion of their resources in research and development when compared with single plant independent firms. These results show that small independent firms appear to devote a similar proportion of their resources to research and development when compared with their multi plant counterparts.

Table 4.6

Proportion of total workforce employed in research and development
by organisational status

Percentage of workforce in research and development	Single plant		Multi plant	
	N	%*	N	%*
0-4	13	44.8	16	55.2
5-9	13	38.2	21	61.8
10-19	18	58.1	13	41.9
20+over	4	50.0	4	50.0
Total	48	47.1	54	52.9

chi square = 2.2   not significant at the p = 0.05 level
* Proportion of total respondents in any given percentage of
  workforce in research and development size category

It is not possible to assess the extent to which these results can
be applied generally. It would certainly appear to be the case that
firms within MLH 354, due to the high technology involved in their
activities, place especial emphasis on the need for research and
development. Indeed, of the 102 plants visited, only 7 had no
research and development department and of these 3 were receiving
technical information from parent organisations abroad and one
received information from a research and development department
elsewhere in Britain. Thus only 3 plants had no established
access to new technical information, 2 of these being optical
instrument manufacturers, a specialised area of MLH 354 with a
mature and established form of technology.

4.4. THE ORGANISATION OF MANAGEMENT

The number of senior executives operating at any given plant location
may prove a useful insight into the effects of size and organisational
structure upon the tasks of top management. Luttrell (1962) and
Townroe (1971), in their studies of broad sectors of relocating
industry, both mention the extensive use of factory managers in
small and recently relocated branch factories. It would appear that,
for many industrial sectors, the day to day running of such an
establishment is within the capabilities of a non-executive manager.

It was deemed of organisational relevance to this study to assess
whether such a phenomenon as factory manager applied to MLH 354,
considering the high degree of technical and administrative
complexity and independence evidenced in other spheres of organisation.
It was also considered to be of interest whether there was a strong
relationship between total employment size and the number of directors
or senior executives in control at any given plant. It would appear
that, on cursory examination, there should be a proportionate
increase in senior executive staff with an increase in total
employment size within the plant.

A qualification of the results of this section must be made in
that, as discussed by Townroe (1971), the semantic problem of
defining the meaning of terms exhibits great variability between
organisations. For example, the term managing director normally

27

applies to the senior director of a company board. However, in a limited number of cases, the term managing director is applied to a post that is, in effect, plant manager (usually in very large firms). In other circumstances, the term managing director is applied to a proprietor who, for limited liability and tax reasons, prefers to form a limited company, with perhaps other token directors (usually in very small firms). However, these instances apply to a small minority of establishments and aggregate results minimise any effect these anomalous cases might produce.

The existence of plant managers within the sample was easily assessed. Of the 102 plants visited, only 10 had a single managing director. None of the 10 establishments actually referred to the single senior executive as plant manager, though objectively this was in fact the case. Of these 10 establishments with only one managing director, three were branch factories. Interestingly, these three plants were among the largest in the total sample (550, 600 and 1,500 employees respectively). Although not managing directors in the true boardroom sense, these executives were not, due to the obvious amount of autonomy they displayed, the highly subordinate managers referred to by Luttrell and Townroe.

The branch manager in the non-senior executive sense was therefore absent from the MLH 354 study sample. Indeed, a simple assessment of the relative number of senior staff operating in the 13 headquarters and 41 branch factories within the total sample revealed that the mean number of directors for headquarters was four, while the figure for branch plants was six. These figures again lend weight to the growing impression of great autonomy displayed by branch factories within MLH 354.

Size of plant did not prove to be any more effective in determining the number of senior executives employed at sample plants. A correlation performed upon the data using employment size as the independent variable and the number of directors or senior managers as the dependent variable produced an insignificant correlation coefficient of $r = 0.2182$. The previously mentioned large plants with single 'managing directors' did not help the correlation to produce a significant coefficient, but other factors contributed to the weakness of the relationship. One establishment with 20 employees boasted seven directors. This particular firm had adopted a progressive policy towards its senior staff and was prepared to admit employees at board level as a means of creating a constructive work environment, and of providing incentives to earn company profits.

Apart from the obvious influence of family businesses often providing as many directors as there were family members working for the firm, there was the additional importance of small firms with a large proportion of directors who had 'spun off' from a large local firm. Key personnel from the original large firm combine to form a company to produce a product, or range of products, for which they have developed a specialised technical advantage. Such firms frequently possess a large proportion of executives in relation to their total workforces. An example of this phenomenon is Measurement Technology of Luton, a company that was formed as a 'spin off' from the giant George Kent company of the

same town. The four directors of the 20 employee establishment were
all former George Kent employees utilising specialised talents
developed while in the employ of their large neighbour.

The impression gained from a combined assessment of the above
information is complex. Size would not appear to the a determining
factor of the number of directors or senior executives possessed
by establishments. The branch manager, common to many other industrial
sectors, appears irrelevant to MLH 354. An analysis of senior
executives within MLH 354 has again revealed the independence of the
individual establishment in its possession of a generally autonomous
management structure, regardless of size or status.

4.5. MULTI PLANT ORGANISATIONAL STRUCTURE

Under this heading the objectives are twofold; namely to ascertain

1. The total size of the organisation of which the multi
   plant sample establishments are a part
2. Where applicable, the number of other MLH 354 plants
   that exist within the multi plant organisations and to
   discover the proportion of instrument industry
   establishments within these large organisations.

By comparing the results obtained from these two lines of inquiry,
it should be possible to understand the general character of multi
plant organisations but, more specifically, the extent to which
MLH 354 is a central industrial activity for the organisations
of which certain multi plant establishments in the survey sample
are a part. Or, conversely, whether the instrument manufacturing
portion of these large organisations is an insignificant side line.

The size structure of the 54 multi plant sample organisations
is given in Table 4.7 below. This table indicates that 27 (50 per cent)
of the multi plant firms had over nine establishments in their
group, signifying large organisations. These plants constituted
50 per cent of the sub-sample and 26.5 per cent of the total sample
(N = 102). The 27 establishments belonging to large organisations

Table 4.7
Multi plant establishments; number of plants in group

Number of plants in group	Responses	
	Number	%
2	9	16.7
3	4	7.4
4	6	11.1
5	4	7.4
6	1	1.9
7	2	3.7
8	1	1.8
9	0	0.0
over 9	27	50.0
N =	54	100.0

were then analysed to ascertain if the organisations to which they
belonged possessed a large number of instrument making plants within
their sphere of operations. Table 4.8 presents the results of the
question concerning the number of plants in the multi plant
organisations which produced MLH 354 products. Of the 27 firms
with over 9 plants in their organisation, 11 had more than 5 plants
of the group within MLH 354. This represents 20.4 per cent of the
multi plant sample (N = 54) and 10.8 per cent of the total sample
(N = 102).

Table 4.8
Firms with over nine plants in group; number of plants within MLH 354

Number of plants in MLH 354	Number of firms with more than nine plants in group
1	4
2	2
3	4
4	2
5	4
6	2
7	2
8	0
over 8	7
	N = 27

The figures in Table 4.8 suggest the importance of a few multi
plant (often multi sector) giants. The 11 firms with over 9 plants
within MLH 354 included such companies as Ferranti, Thorn, EMI,
George Kent and Rank. No figures exist to permit a direct measure
of the percentage contribution of these firms to the total output
of MLH 354, but the above information on the extent of their
organisational strength within the present sample may, to some
extent, act as a general surrogate. Smaller multi plant organisations
accounted for the small number of firms with all their plants operating
within MLH 354 (i.e. 12 companies, 11.8 per cent of the total sample).
The complete data is given in Table 4.9

Table 4.9
Size of organisations with all their plants operating in MLH 354

Organisation size (number of plants)	Number of survey sample organisations with all their plants in MLH 354
2	4
3	2
4	3
5	2
6	1
7	0
8	0
9	0
over 9	0
	N = 12

4.6. TAKEOVER AND MERGER ACTIVITY

For the successful firm the presence of entrepreneurial enterprise
and capital strength may combine to produce a drive towards the
expansion of company operations. This expansion may take at least
two forms:

1. Construction of new, or the expansion of existing,
   premises
2. Acquisition of another existing production organisation
   by means of takeover or merger activity.

In this section attention will be given to the second alternative.
The degree of takeover or merger activity exhibited by sample plants
will be used as a general measure of the industrial strength and
vitality of MLH 354. However, before embarking upon a detailed
analysis of takeover and merger activity, it should again be stressed
that MLH 354 is strongly characterised by a small average establishment
size. The largest plant in the survey sample (1,650 employees)
would not be considered large in many other sectors of industry.
Hence, the general intra or inter industrial sector power that may
be displayed by MLH 354 plants must be constrained by the generally
small size of plants in this industry.

Further, it must be emphasised that the term 'giant' mentioned
previously in this chapter mainly applies to organisations that have
earned this status in industrial sectors separate from MLH 354.
Later in this section an attempt will be made to ascertain the
extent to which the large size of such organisations can be related
to their MLH 354 activities, but it should not be automatically
assumed that either a large plant within MLH 354, or the large
organisation to which it may belong, has been created from
instrument industry profits.

4.7. THE EFFECT OF MULTI SECTOR COMPANIES ON MLH 354

It is useful at this point to introduce a consideration of the multi
sectoral characteristics of many of the organisations that have a
proportion of their activity within the present MLH 354 sample. It
is especially pertinent to bear in mind the phenomenon outlined by
McNee (1974) where an industrial organisation, already successful in
its original sphere of technology, with a history of horizontal
acquisitions within its own industrial sector, may decide to
diversify its operations into new areas of technology largely
unknown to the decision making capabilities of existing executives.

These comments are particularly relevant to MLH 354. The 54 multi
plant firm executives indicated that takeover or merger activity
had influenced their plant in the manner indicated by Table 4.10.
Of the 34 establishments that had been subject to takeover or
merger activity, 33 had been absorbed, with only one merger. These
striking results suggest that MLH 354 does not act as a sectoral
platform from which expansion may take place. It was considered
of further interest to ascertain whether the acquiring organisations
were expanding from a strong MLH 354 base.

31

Table 4.10
Organisational change

	Number of plants	Proportion of multi plant sample (%)	Proportion of total sample (%)
Takeovers	33	61.1	32.3
Mergers	1	1.9	1.0
No change	20	37.0	19.6
Total	54	100.0	52.9

If the acquiring organisations did not have their main activities within MLH 354, then the behaviour explained by McNee in his hypothetical example may have been in evidence. McNee (1974,p56) states 'The leaders of Gismo-Gadget realised that the most important single asset of the merged firm was not listed at all on the company accounting books. Things listed on the books (facilities owned, supplies accounts receivable, reserves) were all less significant really, than something rather more intangible, the reality of a "going concern" '. Indeed, it would be no surprise if an acquiring organisation, entering MLH 354 for the first time, would not wish to replace key personnel in an acquired plant, since the instrument industry exhibits a high degree of unique complex technology. The generally short production runs or custom built types of production contribute greatly to the individual specialised knowledge of management. In the purchasing of specialised materials, their skilled assembly and the final meeting of customer's separate and precise needs, the MLH 354 firm's value largely lies in the knowledge and skills of the total workforce of any given plant.

Support for McNee's general assertion would be gained from an analysis of the acquiring organisations to derive what proportion of the group's total activities could be included under Minimum List Heading 354. The plants that had been acquired were related to their acquiring organisation's size, and the number of establishments within MLH 354 were expressed as a percentage of the total number of plants within the complete group. Organisations were considered to be MLH 354 dominated if over 50 per cent of their total establishments were within MLH 354. The results of this analysis are given below (Table 4.11).

Table 4.11
Proportion of acquiring organisations involved in MLH 354

	Organisations with more than 50% of establishments in MLH 354	Organisations with less than 50% of establishments in MLH 354
Acquired establishments	5	29

N = 34

The figures in this table show that the acquiring organisations are not predominantly concerned with MLH 354 production. By virtue of the lack of acquisitions initiated by sample firms, and the non

32

MLH 354 base of 29 of the 34 acquiring organisations, it would appear that the scientific and industrial instruments industry does not provide a level of financial strength to enable organisations based purely on MLH 354 to expand, as described by McNee (1974), into other technological areas. Further support for the low rate of expansion from a MLH 354 base is provided by the additional statistic that among the five organisations with over 50 per cent of their production plants within MLH 354, the total number of plants in these firms was smaller than that in the less than 50 per cent group. Indeed, the reverse would appear true that large groups of companies, predominantly occupied in other technological fields, have bought their way into MLH 354 with profits made in other sectors.

McNee's view that large organisations tend to purchase going concerns when expansion into a new sphere of industrial operation is initiated and technical knowledge is lacking, is considered specially pertinent to MLH 354. It has been shown that acquiring organisations do not, in general, have their main activities within MLH 354. Thus, it may be tentatively suggested that these organisations are purchasing establishments outside their own technologically secure sphere of knowledge.

This would appear a logical general assumption, but it must be remembered that, although 27 firms had less than 50 per cent of their establishments in MLH 354, for a few giant organisations, the actual number of MLH 354 plants was reasonably high. However, these firms were in a minority (i.e. only six of the 27 firms with less than 50 per cent of their activities in MLH 354 had more than five plants in the instruments' industry. Further, it is highly unlikely, due to the previously outlined sophistication of MLH 354, that a large acquiring organisation with a MLH 354 background would seek to disrupt the organisational and technical management structure of an acquired instrument industry firm.

All the takeovers were completed within the past 20 years, 25 (73.5 per cent) of these acquisitions having taken place within the past 10 years. However, dispite the contemporary nature of the majority of these takeovers, the 34 firms that have been subjected to this major organisational change do not show any added signs of disruption in control at plant level, when compared with remaining sample firms. The general characteristics of an absence of plant managers, freedom to purchase and contract and internalised research and development and transport facilities, displayed generally throughout the study sample, was continued within the acquired firms.

Takeovers, when they occurred, seemed rarely to be traumatic affairs. For example, the statement by the managing director of a sample firm that had been taken over by a USA competitor, exemplified the often loose knit character of such acquisitions. He said that the directors (his brother and himself) had sold 51 per cent of the company shares to an American competitor. For this theoretical loss of control, the company gained greatly increased financial support, potential technical assistance, plus the agency for the USA parent's larger range of products. Significantly, top management had not changed, and the only areas of contact with the parent company were on the availability of finance, and joint strategy towards product markets.

The evidence on the effect of multi sector companies on the control of MLH 354 establishments has continued to confirm the high level of independence of individual instrument plants within multi sector firms. The weakness of MLH 354 in the field of takeovers and mergers has been clearly shown. Technological complexity, short production runs (often custom built jobs) and high labour costs, all suggest that large profits are difficult to secure in instrument production. This, in turn, must affect the capacity of MLH 354 firms to produce the kind of funds required for the purchasing of other businesses.

Conversely, electronic firms (e.g. Thorn, Rank and GEC), having made considerable profits in other, less technically sophisticated, areas of the electronics industry, are able to acquire going concerns within MLH 354 with profits made in totally different technological areas of production. As previously stated, there is little evidence to support the theory that instrument firms are acquired as a means of internalising externalities for the purchasing organisation. The independence factor emerges again in that suppliers and markets are not, after acquisition, suddenly switched to within group companies.

The increased merger activity of the past ten years supports a view of the general trend in manufacturing industry towards a rationalisation of the number of single enterprises into larger, more complex organisations. To exemplify the degree of diversity evidenced by a large company organisation, the 'family tree' of Plantation Holdings Ltd. is reproduced in Figure 4.3.
Areas of activity within the company range from rubber plantations to scientific instruments. The instruments division was created by the purchase of two going concerns, Shandon Southern Instruments Ltd. and Bryans Southern Instruments Ltd. The previous experience of Plantation Holdings had been in the sphere of rubber plantations, and therefore the purchase of a going concern incorporates the knowledge of the complete company personnel.

Such a diverse span of company technology has a major advantage in that a more stabilised level of total profits can be produced through diversification. The strategy of 'not putting all your eggs in one basket' would appear applicable here. But, as a consequence of this diversification, it is not surprising that, at the individual plant level (e.g. Shandon Southern Products Ltd., Figure 4.3), the degree of individual plant executive control is high. As McNee (1974) has stated, the expansion of an organisation often involves the loss of relevant information by headquarters at branch plant level, making decisions essential at the local branch, where the information relevant to the decision is available.

4.8.   FOREIGN CONTROL

Table 4.12 indicates the extent to which foreign control is present in the study sample. Twelve of the 102 establishments (11.8 per cent) were owned by foreign organisations. This rather low proportion may reflect the strength of the British instruments industry and its ability to keep a hold on the home market.

Group Organisation

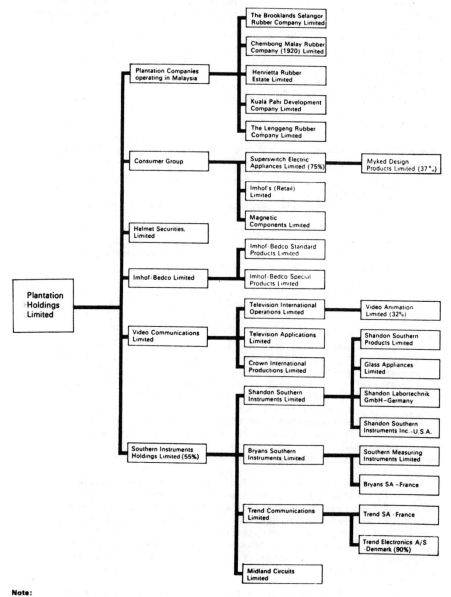

Figure 4.3 The organisational structure of a large diversified firm

Table 4.12
Location of control

Headquarter location	Single plant establishments	Multi plant establishments
Britain	46	44
USA	1*	8
FGR	1*	0
Switzerland	0	1
Netherlands	0	1
Total	48	54

*One plant in Britain   N = 102

For the foreign company wishing to penetrate the British market four main strategies may be adopted. These are:

1. Direct export and the establishment of agency facilities either with company personnel or through an associate company. This will facilitate sales, spare parts and service.
2. Arrange for the products to be manufactured in Britain by an independent company under licence. Sales and spare parts are catered for under the arrangement, but profits to the innovating firm are reduced.
3. Establish a branch factory in Britain
4. Take over an established, technologically similar firm, improving or modifying existing products and adding the range of products originally intended for sale in the national market of the acquired firm.

The strategy adopted will depend upon a multitude of economic and political factors and is comprehensively covered by Blackbourn (1974) in respect of American firms locating in Europe. A critical factor in deciding the extent of commitment to a particular market will be the volume of trade developed, or envisaged, by the foreign company. Low volume of exports would favour strategies one or two above, while a considerable flow of products into a foreign market might necessitate strategies three or four. Choice between strategies three or four may depend on many factors, but major, mutually exclusive advantages exist for both approaches.

A new factory may be eligible for government assistance and Blackbourn considers this to be a significant attraction for American firms locating in Britain and Belguim where government incentives are relatively high . However the purchase of a going concern alleviates many of the critical difficulties of understanding national business practices, laws and general behaviour. This additional manufacturing facility can be purchased fully staffed and in production from the outset.

Of the 12 MLH 354 plants under foreign control, three were new factories (strategy three), while the remaining nine plants had been purchased as going concerns (strategy four - see Table 4.13). The predominance of this approach is not surprising in view of the difficulties involved in staffing a factory in a sector of industry where the majority of the labour force is skilled and in short supply. While disaggregation of the main sample means a subsequent reduction in the validity of any conclusions that may be drawn from a 12 plant sub-sample, it does appear that especially for American firms, the most popular method of marketing a product that has been developed in the home market (and is therefore of low extra cost when sold or produced abroad) is to purchase an existing company in Britain. By doing so, the purchasing foreign firm may slowly add to or replace the company products with its own. No production is lost in the process and the acquired plant continues to earn regular profits.

Table 4.13
Location strategy of foreign firms

Headquarter location	Establishment of new factory	Purchase of a going concern
USA	2	7
FGR	1	0
Switzerland	0	1
Netherlands	0	1
Total	3	9

N = 12

4.9. CONCLUSION

By the observation of selected aspects of the organisational behaviour of MLH 354 plants, a strong general level of independence has been established. Single plant independent firms show great autonomy in their drive to be self sufficient in technical information. Multi plant branch factories give evidence of autonomy in their relationships with their controlling headquarters. This autonomy stems from the high technology and specialised nature of many of the MLH 354 plant's operations, which ensures that decision making must remain at plant level.

The complexity of the types of products, and the vast range of variations under major product headings manufactured within MLH 354, may contribute to the general lack of activity exhibited by MLH 354 firms towards takeovers and mergers. While the value of goods produced is always high, productivity per worker is frequently low due to the non-standardised nature of products and the inability to introduce permanent production runs. Firms may offer many instruments in their catalogues that they do not regularly produce, but would supply to customers' specification if ordered. Further, the technical specifications of many products are consistently being improved, thus necessitating the need for constant revisions and improvements in design. Technical specification, in many cases, is as important as price in a competitive market.

For all these reasons, the ability to expand rapidly may well be restricted owing to the inability of the majority of firms within the industry to make the standardisation and economies of scale that return high profits. The figures given on takeovers (Table 4.10) must reflect this inability among MLH 354 firms to use the

instruments' industry as a basis for acquisition. Organisations
based in other, often similar, fields of technology, such as
electronics, have been able to purchase their way into MLH 354.

However, it has been noted that, once purchased, there is no
evidence to suggest that the organisation of the acquired firm
markedly changes. The incursion by organisations external to MLH 354
would not generally be an attempt to vertically integrate a network
of production, since input and output linkage interaction is minimal.
More probably, the acquisition of MLH 354 firms is the result of
an attempt by firms from other industrial sectors to diversify
their activities in order to be better placed to resist slumps in
any given market.

5 Information

Only in recent years has the spatial availability of information
been exposed as an important consideration in the location behaviour
of industrial organisations. Theoretical and empirical work by
geographers (Pred and Tornqvist 1973, Goddard 1978) has stressed
the uneven distribution of available information in a national
context. The scope of such studies frequently encompasses a
consideration of the total intake of information that is extracted
from the surrounding environment by both manufacturing and tertiary
organisations (Thorngren 1970).

This chapter is concerned with the acquisition of a particular
type of information directly related to production. MLH 354 is an
industry particularly sensitive to the rapid technological changes
that affect its products. For many instrument firms an up to date
specification is as important as price in determining sales, and
the long term viability of the individual firm. Consequently, the
acquisition of technical information relating to product design
and production, through their contact with local research
establishments might be expected to be the most significant
locational constraint on information gathering for instrument
industry firms.

A further comment on the character of the technical information
received by MLH 354 establishments is relevant here. At a general
level, as adopted by many studies of information flows, little
distinction is made between information that is readily available in
proportion to the amount of search undertaken and highly confidential
information that is not widely available. This is no surprise,
since most information obtained by industrial organisations is from
widely available sources. The acquisition of such knowledge depends
upon the amount of resources the individual organisation wishes to
devote to the search process. There is considerable agreement on
this proposition (Cyert and March 1962, Webber 1968, Pred and
Tornqvist 1973). Information search activity will vary between
industrial organisations and may range from the simple to the
sophisticated, often influenced by the size of the organisation.
Rees (1974) has shown the differing degrees of search activity
displayed by 10 large companies with regard to relocation behaviour.

However, in the case of MLH 354, the technical information
required by firms, relating to production, is not generally available
in proportion to the amount of search activity. This information
is concerned with the acquisition of high technology innovations that
improve existing products or invent new products, to give advantage
over competitors. The desirability of an item of technical
information is determined by its exclusiveness. It is because

the value of innovations lie in their potential monopolisation
by a given firm that such a high proportion of plants within the
MLH 354 sample possess their own research and development departments.
As previously stated 95 (93.1 per cent) of sample plants have their
own research and development departments. While background information
(e.g. technical reports, information on the performance of components)
can be obtained from technical libraries or academic, government or
private research establishments, exclusive rights to new innovations
can only be secured by research and development within the confines
of the individual factory or organisation. Figure 5.1 represents,
in a diagrammatic form, a general view of information gathering,
as it applies to MLH 354 production.

In this figure, total acquired information is shown as evolving
from three sources, government, private and academic. For two of
these sources, government and private, finance may also be obtained.
The degree of success in finding the desired information and finance
will largely depend, as stated above, on the research investment.
Any information and finance obtained will then support the individual
plant's research and development department where general technical
background information is adapted to the specialist needs of the
individual establishment.

5.2. SOURCES OF TECHNICAL INFORMATION

At the national level, various organisations exist to promote
innovation within industry. Notably, the Production Engineering
Research Association (PERA), the National Research and Development
Corporation (NRDC), and, to a lesser extent, specialist departments
of universities. Such organisations offer a range of differing
technical and financial facilities that may be of use to a firm with
an innovative idea that requires technical or financial exploitation.
The government backed NRDC is prepared to provide financial
assistance in the development of new technology, while PERA, an
organisation set up by private industry with government assistance,
offers a range of technical advice on subjects varying from labour
management to technical problems. Advice is subject to the payment
of a membership fee.

These facilities, amalgamated with many other private consultancy
facilities of varying size, ranging from large consultancy firms
to individual members of university staffs, are available to senior
executives of MLH 354 firms. However, the degree of interaction
initiated by these firms may be restricted by the generally small
average size of companies within the industry. There is a real problem
in that much of the assistance offered is of a type appropriate to
large scales of production, and is thus inappropriate for a very
small firm with limited output.

This situation must also be exacerbated by the psychological
resistance of many small firm executives to the use of outside
consultancy advice on running their businesses. Resistance to
external advice in making business decisions derives from two major
stimuli. First, the managing director of a small firm often needs
much convincing that an outside consultant could assess the intricate
functioning of his business more usefully than internal company

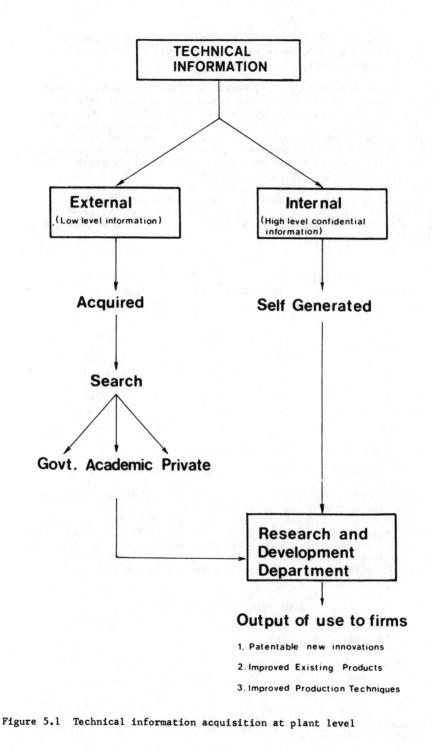

Figure 5.1   Technical information acquisition at plant level

executives. Second, there is no guarantee that after incurring
the costs of employing consultants, the undertaken 'improvements'
will bring about improved efficiency and profits.

Questions were devised to ascertain the use of consultancy advice.
If the above argument holds, then consultancy should be less evident
in smaller sample plants, since the strong link between small plant
size and single plant independent firm status (Table 4.5) has been
established. When asked if consultancy advice had been obtained,
the 102 sample establishments divided almost equally in their responses,
with 46 (45.1 per cent) plants replying affirmatively, and 56 (54.9 per
cent) plants indicating that no use was made of consultancy advice.
With regard to the size characteristics of the two sub-samples,
Table 5.1 indicates that there is a strong relationship between
small plant size and the group of establishments with no consultancy
contacts (the chi square test was significant at the $p = 0.001$ per cent
level).

Table 5.1
Size of plant by use of consultancy advice

Plant size (number of employees)	Used consultancy advice		Did not use consultancy advice	
	N	%*	N	%*
1-19	3	33.3	6	66.7
20-49	10	32.3	21	67.7
50-99	9	40.9	13	59.1
100-199	7	58.3	5	41.7
200-499	8	50.0	8	50.0
500-999	7	77.8	2	22.2
1000+over	2	66.7	1	33.3
Total	46	45.1	56	54.9

chi square $= 14.7$ $p = 0.001$ per cent

* proportion of respondents in any given size category

With regard to the 47 plants making use of consultancy advice, a
further question attempted to discover the broad areas of
plant operation in which the advice was received. The categories
were investment (including personnel administration), technical and
location, and covered general areas where consultancy might be useful
to company decision making. The result of this further inquiry
is given in Table 5.2. Although it must be stressed that the

Table 5.2
Consultancy advice (by type)*

Investment (including personnel management)		Technical		Location	
N	%	N	%	N	%
19	40.4	33	70.2	1	2.1

N = 47

*Figures total 53 (112.7 per cent) as certain plants acknowledged
more than one category

42

figures in this table are concerned with less than half the study sample, the use of consultancy for technical purposes predominates and supports the general impression of a high emphasis on technical innovation and improved product design.

Table 5.3 indicates that the main source of consultancy information was private, probably reflecting the often informal and personal nature of much consultancy, especially for small and medium sized firms. Such consultancy arrangements are frequently based upon personal contacts and involve individuals rather than consultancy firms. Only brief comment will be made here on the reaction of firms to locational consultancy, since a chapter is devoted to relocation later in the study. Suffice it to state that 18 sample plants had relocated within the past five years and several more had considered or were in the process of considering a move. The lack of consultation on this topic, for which very little previous experience could be called upon, is striking but not altogether surprising in the light of other research (Townroe 1971).

Table 5.3
Source of consultancy advice by type of advice

	Investment (including personnel)	Technical	Location
Government	1	4	0
Private	16	23	1
Both	2	6	0
Totals	19	33	1

N = 53

5.3. LOCAL INFORMATION CONTACTS AND LOCATION

In his study of the instruments industry in the USA Gibson (1970) re-affirmed the belief generally held in the United States that large university complexes (e.g. Massachusetts Institute of Technology, the University of California and Stanford University) act as particularly attractive areas for the birth and growth of instrument firms. Gibson stressed the research and development services provided on a contract basis by many of these institutions, thus providing a highly localised rich supply of technical information of a type similar to the self-generated, highly confidential knowledge shown as internal to British firms in Figure 5.1. This high quality external research and development would appear to afford advantages for firms located in areas rich in such facilities. Deuterman, in her survey of the science based industries of Boston and Philadelphia also stressed the local informational advantage provided by the universities of these two areas (Deuterman 1966).

Having established that areas of high research activity are strong locational attractions for science based and high technology industries in the United States, it would seem logical to test the locational influence of local external technical information contacts on British MLH 354 plants. Table 5.4 shows the results of a question on the existence and type of information links with local (i.e. within

43

30 miles) research establishments. The most striking statistic in the table is that 37 (36.3 per cent) establishments had no local research establishment contacts at all. This would appear to weaken the hypothesis that research establishments act as a locational attraction to MLH 354 production. These 37 establishments were analysed to detect any common feature which might explain their lack of local research contacts. Chi square tests to measure the influence of plant size and multi plant/single plant status yielded no significance at the p = 0.05 per cent level. A further test, to ascertain if the lack of contact with research establishments was a result of relative spatial isolation, was no more useful.

Table 5.4
Local research establishment contacts

Type of contact	North West		South East		Total	
	N	%	N	%	N	%
Academic	7	19.4	6	9.1	13	12.8
Government	3	8.3	6	9.1	9	8.8
Private	1	2.7	3	4.6	4	3.9
Academic/ Government	6	16.7	9	13.6	15	14.7
Academic/ Private	2	5.5	2	3.0	4	3.9
Government/ Private	0	0.0	3	4.5	3	2.9
Academic/ Government/ Private	4	11.1	13	19.7	17	16.7
None	13	36.2	24	36.4	37	36.3
Totals	36	100.0	66	100.0	102	100.0

The most probable explanation for the behaviour of plants with no local technical information contacts results from the attitudes of their top administrators. All forms of production within MLH 354 would benefit from regular research establishment interaction. All sample plants possessed in their local area at least one academic, government or private research establishment which could have afforded technical assistance. No spatial bias existed in favour of the peripheries of the two regions with regard to the firms not interacting with local research establishments. Hence this lack of interaction must indicate a lack of enterprise, or lack of a perceived need on the part of the executives concerned, rather than the non-availability of potentially relevant information.

Of the 65 (63.7 per cent) plants boasting local research establishment contacts, academic contacts were the most frequent, followed closely by government contacts, leaving private contacts a poor third (Table 5.5). This table is a simplification of Table 5.4, which facilitates greater clarity in the observation of the three forms of contact. The popularity of academic and government contacts almost certainly reflects the relative abundance of such establishments and is further stimulated by the free nature of much of the information obtained from these sources.

Table 5.5
Local research establishment contacts

Type of contact	North West		South East		Total	
	N	%	N	%	N	%
Academic	19	48.7	30	36.6	49	40.5
Government	13	33.3	31	37.8	44	36.4
Private	7	18.0	21	25.6	28	23.1
	39	100.0	82	100.0	121	100.0

Although 65 firms acknowledged local research establishment contacts, a subsequent question was put to respondents in order to gauge the strength of such information flows. For if, as writers in the USA have suggested, areas with technologically important research establishments act as attracting forces upon the instrument industry, then certainly the North West and South East planning regions should display these characteristics if they are to be detected anywhere in Britain, given the national distribution of research establishments and the predominance of the instruments industry in these two planning regions.

When asked if the loss of information from local research establishments would cause serious difficulty if the plant were forced to relocate out of the region, 55 of the establishments with local research establishment contacts (84.6 per cent) responded negatively. If this statistic is taken with the previously emphasised fact that 37 plants had no local research contacts at all, there remains nine plants (8.8 per cent) in the 102 establishment sample which deemed local research establishments of significant locational importance. Hence, these data do not support the United States evidence with regard to instrument firms' dependence upon local research establishments. Some general conclusions and an attempt to explain this specific discrepancy are presented below.

5.4. CONCLUSIONS

In concluding this section it is useful to return to Figure 5.1 and the discussion of exclusive versus generally available information. This method of viewing information access is particularly appropriate in explaining the above results. The lack of serious location influencing links between industrial firms and research establishments is almost certainly reflected in the low level technical complexity of MLH 354 research establishment contacts.

Unlike the United States examples, where Gibson (1970) was able to stress the importance of contract research carried on by universities, British universities do not generally offer these high level facilities. The large proportion of public sector funding of universities in Britain contrasts with the academic scene in the USA, where much university research funding derives from private industry. Hence, the degree of commercially orientated contract research is reduced in the British case.

Major universities of high technical repute in the two survey planning regions were approached and inquiries were made as to their provision of research assistance and facilities and their attitudes to confidential contract research. Examples of the general attitude adopted by universities in Britain are provided by Imperial College (London) and the University of Manchester Institute of Science and Technology (UMIST). Representatives of both establishments stated that, in certain instances, research and development of a collaborative nature had been undertaken, but no formal machinery existed for the promotion of such services and arrangements appeared to be rather 'ad hoc'. It was acknowledged that problems may occur over confidentiality and the resultant patents that may evolve from joint projects between the university and industrial firms. Further, since the main objective of a university is the pursuit of knowledge 'per se', areas of common interest with industrial firms are mainly coincidental, rather than representing an attempt to match the topics of academic research to the specific needs of industry.

For all the above reasons, the degree of research collaboration that exists between MLH 354 firms and universities is minimal, save where specialist firms are actually producing scientific apparatus for university departments. The high level of academic contacts shown in Table 5.5 reflects, in the main, the acquisition of generally available low level information which is dependent on the amount of search undertaken (e.g. from libraries). This would explain the negative response to the question asking if a relocation would seriously affect and disrupt contacts with local research establishments. The obvious inference is that the type of information gained locally is of low importance or could be equally easily obtained elsewhere.

This contrasts with the situation in the USA where the existence of research contracts for the confidential development of new products and processes between industrial firms and spatially concentrated research organisations establishes a far firmer high level technical information link, that is spatially unique and hence, a strong locational constraint upon firms. For, in the competitive markets of high technology industry, it is information leading to the technical development of improved products which give advantage over competitors that is the most valuable, and consequently the most guarded, information. MLH 354 firms generally internalise their sources of such information in their own research and development departments due to the general absence of contract research facilities. Contacts with other sources of research and development information are of a low level and supportive in nature.

6 Transport

6.1. INTRODUCTION

Both major schools of traditional location theory have encouraged
subsequent location theorists to approach the consideration of the
effects of transport on location as predominantly a function of
costs stemming from an analysis of weight and distance. Weber (1909)
and Lösch (1954) with the 'location triangle' and 'demand cone'
respectively, viewed the locational importance of transport as
simply a manifestation of the cost of movement of industrial goods,
be they inputs to the industrial plant or products dispatched
to the market.

More recently, with the increased share held by high value added
goods as a proportion of total national industrial output, the
importance of transport costs, and thereby transport as a location
factor, has generally been viewed as of decreasing significance.
Fulton and Hoch (1959, p58) crystallise this view by arguing that
transport costs '...are a paramount consideration when selecting a
location for a new blast furnace or cement mill but, in direct
contrast, a hundred per cent variation in total freight costs could
be completely disregarded in the choice of sites for a manufacturer
of precision instruments, fountain pens, etc.'.

This chapter is concerned with the transport used for the dispatch
of goods from MLH 354 plants, since, save in a very small number of
cases, the transport costs of delivering raw materials to the
individual plant is borne by the supplier. For the instrument makers
of MLH 354, the proportion of transport costs related to total costs
is indeed small. Bayliss and Edwards(1970), using 1963 industrial
census data, indicated that the cost of transport for scientific,
surgical and photographic instruments (1958 classification) was a
mere 1.65 per cent of total net output, whereas transport costs
for chalk, clay, sand and gravel extraction equalled 39.78 per cent
of total net value of output. As previously indicated, there was a
change in the types of manufacture included in the minimum list
heading dealing broadly with scientific instruments between 1958
and 1968. However, this change is considered irrelevant here since
all the products subsequently included and excluded are consistently
of high value added and therefore neither the percentage quoted, nor
the present argument, is significantly altered by the change.

However, it should not be asserted that because transport costs
are not important to the location of MLH 354 plants, transport is
of no significance to MLH 354 production. Other factors that cause
variability in the distribution and quality of available transport
facilities may affect the efficiency of firms in different locations.
As Wallace (1974, p25) has stated, '... concentration on transport
costs has led to an unwarranted neglect of other characteristics of

the transport industry which are demonstrably significant to manufacturers, and which are potential sources of spatial variation in linkage patterns'.

It is to a degree paradoxical that the factor which renders transport costs unimportant, namely the generally high value of outputs, is also the cause of the general transport factor that _is_ of crucial importance to MLH 354. Because MLH 354 products are delicate and of high value, the method of transport selected must exhibit three major characteristics:

1. Reliability (the product must reach the customer on time)
2. Security (the product must not be stolen or lost in transit)
3. Safe handling (the product must not be broken on arrival).

All three factors given above are aspects of the same basic imperative in that they all seek to ensure safe delivery of the MLH 354 firm's output. It is not merely the value of the goods that demands such general care, but more critical in many cases is the uniqueness of the delivered product. Many MLH 354 products are custom built; if they are lost or damaged in transit immediate replacement from factory stocks would be impossible. Hence once lost or damaged long delays result while a substitute is built or the damaged article repaired. Because transport costs are such a small proportion of total costs for MLH 354, a wide range of transport services are open to the MLH 354 firm, the spatial ramifications of the choice of transport frequently being more dependent upon safe handling than price.

6.2. INTERNAL ROAD TRANSPORT FACILITIES

Edwards (1970, p268) has noted 'Own transport is preferred in industries which produce .... fragile high value commodities, for example scientific instruments, radios and components, furniture'. This study confirms that such an assertion applies to MLH 354 production. Of the 102 establishments visited in this survey, 74 (72.5 per cent) possessed their own transport facilities, a considerable proportion when viewed in the context of the generally small size of plants within the sample. Edwards, in mentioning fragility, has highlighted the importance of safe handling for firms distributing high value added delicate goods. Transport is crucial in that, if not properly organised, it can be a source of friction between vendor and customer. In extreme cases of loss, damage or late delivery, total loss of valued business may be caused to the individual firm. Hence, by the internalisation of transport facilities whenever possible, the firm secures total control over the general quality of delivery.

Further, the sale of many MLH 354 products involves installation as part of the sales contract. In these instances, installation engineers frequently deliver the product to the customer concerned. This practice is a result of the highly complex nature of the technology involved but has a beneficial transport side effect for

firms who undertake this method of product installation. In other
cases, where the firm is large enough to maintain a sales force of
representatives with cars, and the products are small, delivery may
be effected by salesmen in the normal course of customer visits.

The preference of firms within MLH 354 for internal means of
effecting deliveries is most marked. As a general rule, resort to
external means of delivery are only sought after internal
possibilities have been exhausted. The popularity of internalised
transport has important spatial ramifications to be examined later
in this section. However, Table 6.1 indicates the extent to which
the 74 plants with their own transport facilities use them to
distribute their output. The figures show that, although the
internalisation of transport facilities is high, there remains
considerable scope for the use of external road transport.

Table 6.1
Plants with own transport facilities

Proportion of output handled by own vehicles	Number	Percentage of sub-sample	Percentage of total (102)
0-24	27	36.5	26.5
25-49	13	17.6	12.5
50-74	15	20.3	14.7
75-100	19	25.7	18.6

N = 74

6.3. USE OF EXTERNAL TRANSPORT FACILITIES

In situations where internal transport does not exist, or is not
available, the MLH 354 firm must select a mode of transportation
from the range of services offered by specialist transport
organisations. Final choice will depend upon a balancing of many
factors, of which required speed of delivery, safety and the weight
of the product are the most important. It should not be assumed
that, because MLH 354 products are of high value per ton, and transport
costs are largely insignificant, output is consequently of low weight
per consignment. High technology control systems for power stations
can weigh several tons and require specialist packing and handling
from the plant, while at the other extreme certain types of small
instruments can be dispatched through the post. Even within a
minimum list heading displaying such general technical homogeneity
as MLH 354, great diversity may still exist. Bearing in mind the
varying requirements of specific industrial products, the remaining
available external modes of transport are considered below.

Public road transport

The majority of MLH 354 output is dispatched by means of road
transport, either by own vehicles or by professional contractors.
In considering the professional contract transport business, a
useful division can be made between regular services to firms on a
collection and delivery service basis and the specific hiring

49

of a vehicle to deliver a single consignment.

The regular collection and delivery service predominantly applies
to parcels. The main contractors undertaking this area of business
are British Road Services and Securicor. Securicor appears to be
of growing importance in the road delivery of parcel sized products.
Although relatively expensive, the service offers the major benefits
to MLH 354 firms of fast delivery of goods in a safely handled
manner, from both fragility and security viewpoints. Of the sample
plants visited, seven (6.9 per cent) establishments made regular use
of Securicor, and many more mentioned that the service was used
intermittently for special and urgent high value deliveries. Clearly,
for many firms, cost prevents the regular use of such a high level
service.

The use of external transport services for the dispatch of
irregular consignments usually applies to heavy loads which are
beyond the capability of a firm's own transport fleet. The economic
constraint on own transport delivery lies in the inability of firms
with one consignment constituting a part load to compete on a cost
basis with a professional haulier who will 'top up' a large vehicle
with a consignment, adding to other part load consignments from more
than one customer. Moreover, the professional haulier will have
arranged a return load from the area of destination so further
reducing general costs. This phenomenon is described by Wallace (1974)
and was mentioned by several interviewees in this survey.

Rail transport

Generally, rail transport did not appear to represent a popular mode
of dispatching goods to customers. Considerable disenchantment was
expressed regarding the handling quality of rail services. Indeed,
independent figures produced by Bayliss and Edwards (1970) show that,
for a broad range of industrial types, deliveries by rail are
marginally more prone to damage and loss.

Table 6.2
Use of rail transport in MLH 354

Proportion of output handled by rail transport	North West			South East			Total		
	N.	% of sub-sample	% of total sample	N.	% of sub-sample	% of total sample	N.	% of sub-sample	% of total sample
0-24	23	82.1	63.9	34	91.9	51.5	57	87.7	55.9
25-49	1	3.6	2.8	1	2.7	1.5	2	3.1	1.9
50-74	3	10.7	8.3	2	5.4	3.0	5	7.7	4.9
75-100	1	3.6	2.8	-	-	-	1	1.4	1.0
	28			37			65		

Questions were devised to test the importance of rail transport
to MLH 354 establishments. An initial question enquiring if use was
made of rail freight facilities yielded an affirmative response rate
of 65 (63.7 per cent). However, of these plants 57 (55.9 per cent)
used rail transport for less than 25 per cent of their output
(Table 6.2), while only eight establishments (7.8 per cent) used

rail freight for more than 25 per cent of their sales. The Red Star
parcel service constituted a useful part of the rail freight service
but often the absence of a nearby local station, and the need to
deliver and collect from nominated stations, reduced any attractiveness
of the system. Again, general comments on deftness of handling and
loss were discouraging. Use of rail transport would not appear to
be generally suitable for MLH 354 output.

Transport for exports

Since exports are of importance to MLH 354 firms (see Chapter 7 on
linkages), it was considered of interest to ascertain whether the
proximity of a sea port or airport was a considered location factor.
For, although other means of transport must be used in the journey
from factory to export outlet, the close proximity of a port
facilitates a more flexible approach towards exports. This is
particularly true when it is stressed that, for many firms, it is
not merely products but also sales and service staff that need
speedy and efficient port access, in this case almost exclusively to
an airport.

In his study of Heathrow Airport Hoare (1974,p80) asserted that
' ... the factories (valuing their access to Heathrow for freight and
passenger services) are characterised by above average proportions
of research staff or skilled employees, suggesting their concentration
on high value goods'. Thus it should be expected that a port, and
especially an airport facility, would be of importance to MLH 354
firms in view of the industry's high technology products.

Questions devised to test the importance of a local port facility
(i.e. within a 30 mile radius) were put to interviewees. An initial
question ascertaining if a local export outlet existed yielded
affirmative responses from 68 respondents (66.6 per cent). These
68 respondents who possessed a local export outlet were then asked
if they considered it of locational importance. Of this group, 51
(50 per cent) affirmed that the export outlet was of locational
importance, reflecting their regular use of export facilities.
Table 6.3 indicates the type of export outlet by region (i.e. airport
or sea port). Both regions are similar in that they possess
excellent airport and sea port facilities.

Table 6.3
Type of port most frequented by sample plants

	North West		South East		
		Number			Number
Airport	Manchester	19	Heathrow	20	
			Southend	1	
			Gatwick	2	23
Seaport	Liverpool	6	Tilbury	2	
			Dover	1	3
Totals		25			26

N = 51

51

6.4. LOCAL TRANSPORT ECONOMIES AND AGGLOMERATION

In his paper on high value added industry, Pred (1965) asserts that agglomeration in these types of industry will take place because transport costs are insignificant and therefore location at a main central market is facilitated by the absence of a need to locate several plants in the centres of regional market areas, as would be the case for a product where transport costs were high. But this point accepted, if an agglomerated industry were characterised by large numbers of local forward and backward linkages, there should be measurable subsequent local transport economies to be gained when compared with more peripherally based and isolated competitors.

With specific reference to MLH 354, the study sample was tested to ascertain if significant local transport economies existed in the plant's present location. A minority of 26 (25.5 per cent) plants indicated that transport economies were present in their local area. Table 6.4, which divides respondents into zones, indicates the degree of urbanisation for the plants who claimed local transport economies and compares them with the total survey distribution of plants in order to observe possible bias. Zone 1 is an area encompassed by a circle of 15 miles radius based on London and Manchester city centres, while Zone 2 is comprised of the remaining area within the planning region boundary. As might be expected, plants in central connurbations (Zone 1) constituted 19 of the 26 affirmatively responding establishments.

Table 6.4
Location of plants reaping local transport economies

	North West						South East					
	Zone 1		Zone 2		Total		Zone 1		Zone 2		Total	
	N	%	N	%	N	%	N	%	N	%	N	%
Plants with local tran. economies	10	76.9	3	23.1	13	100	9	69.2	4	30.8	13	100
Survey plants in Zone	22	61.1	14	38.9	36	100	25	37.9	41	62.1	66	100

N = 26

Moreover, it is significant that in both the North West and South East the proportion of plants claiming local transport economies is greater than their total survey representation would suggest. While the percentage difference in the North West is more marginal (15.8 per cent), the difference in the South East is most marked (31.3 per cent), almost certainly reflecting the transport economies offered by a capital city location. Thus local transport economies are obtained for this significant minority of sample plants in urban agglomerations. This position would appear reasonable where constant interaction with sub-contractors, suppliers and especially customers, is involved. The manufacturer-customer relationship is important for small firms who supply large local customers who take a high proportion, or all, of total output. Indeed, a minority of small firms in the sample had no marketing infrastructure since the total output of the plant was taken by one or a limited number of large local customers. Further, since the costs of delivery of output most frequently must be absorbed by the manufacturer, these local customer linkages represent a useful cost reduction.

6.5. NATIONAL TRANSPORT COSTS AND LOCATION

As outlined above, instrument firms display a strong tendency to maintain their own transport facilities. This trend is of some locational importance since a good national location means that all markets may be reached most efficiently and at minimum cost. Moreover, reduction of transport distance is especially important for own transport since, in the majority of cases, own vehicles return home empty, it not being possible for the industrial firm to operate in the same way as a specialist haulier who, whenever possible, arranges a full return load to reduce costs (Wallace 1974).

Since analysis is on a bi-regional basis, it is of use to compare results in the two regional sub-samples. A question enquiring if the respondent considered his plant to be optimally positioned from the point of view of minimising national transport costs, with possible responses of well positioned, moderately positioned, poorly positioned and transport costs irrelevant, yielded the results given in Table 6.5. In this question the respondent was asked to ignore the previously considered local area (i.e. within 30 miles of the plant). The most significant difference between the two regions was the considerably larger percentage of establishments in the North West planning region who considered themselves to be well positioned. Further, 5.6 per cent of plants in the North West and 16.7 per cent of plants in the South East considered themselves to be poorly positioned from a national transportation viewpoint.

Table 6.5
Evaluation of location from a national transportation
cost viewpoint

	North West		South East		Total	
	N	%	N	%	N	%
Well positioned	22	61.1	24	36.4	46	45.1
Moderately positioned	4	11.1	18	27.3	22	21.6
Poorly positioned	2	5.6	11	16.6	13	12.7
Transport costs irrelevant	8	22.2	13	19.7	21	20.6

The more central national position of Manchester may explain the more favourable responses towards national transportation in the North West when compared with the South East. This advantage is further enhanced by the excellent system of motorways that can be conveniently entered from the North West (e.g. M62, M6-M1, M5). Indeed, one North Western respondent, located in the Oldham district, stated that his favourable national transport location was the single most important factor affecting his business.

A fundamental national transport problem for South Eastern plants is London itself. This huge urban area, although of great value in many respects, acts as a serious impediment to speedy transport linkages to the Midlands and the North for firms south and south east of the River Thames and its estuary. Of the 11 South Eastern plants that considered their location poor from a national transportation viewpoint, nine were situated south or south east of London. The two remaining plants, although north of London in the Acton area near the North Circular Road, considered local congestion so bad as to eliminate any advantage that the nearby southern end of the M1 motorway might hold for national distribution. The majority of establishments positioned north of London considered themselves to be either well or moderately positioned near the major market of London itself, but not inhibited by congestion from speedily reaching the national markets of the Midlands and the North.

Significantly, only 21 (20.6 per cent) interviewees in the sample thought that transport costs were irrelevant (Table 6.5). This may result from the desire among MLH 354 manufacturers to provide the best possible conditions and service to customers, assuring that high value goods arrive in perfect condition and on time. Own transport, more costly but more reliable, is an example of this phenomenon. Indeed Bayliss and Edwards (1970, p50) have noted that ' ... suppliers were prepared to pay substantially more for the quality of service pertaining to a particular mode, with nearly one third of the consignments not sent by the cheapest form of transport, being sent by a mode that was over 25 per cent more expensive than the cheapest'. Hence it may be that transport costs are of some importance to MLH 354 firms. However, it is not a situation of cost minimisation as would be the case for bulkier low value goods, where transport costs form a large proportion of total costs, but an evaluation in which value for money is the major transport cost criterion, as the MLH 354 firm attempts to deliver high value delicate goods in a manner that reduces damage, loss and delay.

6.6. CONCLUSION

Again, in common with other chapters of this study, it must be observed that the high value added and high technology characteristics of MLH 354 products have had a critical influence on the attitudes of instrument firms towards transport. Pred (1965) has noted that handling costs for high value added products are consistently higher than for low value outputs. Bayliss and Edwards (1970) developed this theme to discover that firms will frequently pay well above minimum rates for transport in order to ensure that products are not merely delivered, but arrive at the chosen destination in a punctual, secure and complete manner. To this end, cost reduction is unimportant, and customer satisfaction is the desired goal. Therefore, there exists a strong tendency for internalised transport facilities to be developed, especially where installation is part of the sales contract.

7 Linkages

7.1. <u>INTRODUCTION</u>

The concept of linkage as a motive force towards agglomeration has
its roots firmly set in the beginnings of location theory. Both
the least cost and market area schools considered the linkages of
production plants to be spatial factors affecting the 'ideal'
location. Weber (1909) considered agglomeration economies derived
from linkage interaction in urban industrial systems a distortive
influence on the least transport cost location. Lösch (1954)
considered final demand linkages (outputs) to be critical to the
most efficient operating location of industrial plants.

Several post war studies have presented results which have
indicated that, for certain highly localised and vertically dis-
integrated industrial types, agglomeration economies are a firm
reality (Wise 1949, Martin 1966, Keeble 1969). But the industries
studied (e.g. gun and jewellery, furniture, clothing manufacture)
were sectors of production that have, for either economic or planning
reasons, tended to be in a state of decline or collapse in their
rapidly changing intra-urban locations. Evidence to support
agglomeration economies for modern types of industry in an age of
large plant size, improved transport and general communications,
seems more difficult to obtain.

The weight of evidence against the agglomerative effects of
linkages on modern industry would appear to be increasing.
Karaska (1969, p368) in his paper on the linkages of the
Philadephia economy was forced to conclude ' ... the overall effect
of the Philadelphia economy upon manufacturing location - within
the context of external, agglomeration economies - appears to be
weak'. Further Moseley and Townroe (1973, p143) in their article
on the analysis of post move linkages of industrial firms from
London, conclude that 'The implications of this study, and the
other linkage studies already referred to, is that local linkages
are not a necessary condition of operation for all but a small
group of companies'. Finally, Gilmour (1974, p341) supports the
above comments by asserting ' ... the agglomerative force of the
complex may be more strongly expressed in the attractions of the
labour force and the strength of linkage with firms that are
involved in service, financial and commercial transactions than
with firms which are directly involved in the interchange of
material inputs and outputs'. Hence, it would appear that
material linkages are of declining significance in determining
the location of modern industries.

However, it would seem logical that, as Lever (1974, p314) has
argued, 'As most chains of production involve additions in value to the
product and reductions in weight, access to markets would be less

important to firms than access to suppliers'. But for MLH 354,
where both inputs and outputs are of generally high value in
comparison with most basic industries, it would be surprising to
find that either markets or material suppliers present a strong
force towards locational inertia. Nonetheless, if one of these
groups of linkages were to be locationally significant, it
seems reasonable to anticipate that proximity to suppliers would
present the greater constraint on location. In the following analysis,
additional care is accordingly taken in the observation of material
supply linkages.

7.2. THE LOCATIONAL IMPORTANCE OF LOCAL MATERIAL INPUTS

An initial question enquiring if local material supplies were so
important that 'serious inconvenience' would be caused by a forced
relocation, revealed that 67 (65.7 per cent)of the 102 sample
plants did not consider their local supply linkages to be locationally
constraining. A more detailed analysis of this question, to
ascertain any urban agglomerative bias in the response pattern, was
devised. Table 7.1 compares the percentage of respondents answering
affirmatively in the urban core areas (Zone 1) with the remainder of
the planning regions, and with the total percentage of all sample
plants in these two areas. Zone 1 is an area encompassed by a
circle of 15 mile radius based on London and Manchester city centres,
while Zone 2 covers the remaining area within the planning region
boundary. There is a slight spatial bias in favour of the urban
cores that is marginal in the North West, but more marked in the
South East. The difference between total and sub-sample percentages
being 5.6 per cent and 8.3 per cent respectively (Table 7.1).

Table 7.1
Distribution of plants with important local supply linkages

	North West						South East					
	Zone 1		Zone 2		Total		Zone 1		Zone 2		Total	
	N	%	N	%	N	%	N	%	N	%	N	%
Plants with important local supply linkages	6	66.7	3	33.3	9	100	12	46.2	14	53.8	26	100
Survey plants in zone	22	61.1	14	38.9	26	100	25	37.9	41	62.1	66	100

N = 35

However, while there appears to be a marginal urban influence on
the locational significance of linkages, it may be deduced generally
that local supply linkages are of low general importance to MLH 354
plants. Hence, the agglomerative force of supply linkages must be
deemed weak, though as the sub-regional data have shown, this effect
is stronger in Zone 1 of the South East planning region. Table 7.2
supports this view by showing the generally low proportion of inputs
derived from local sources. It is interesting to note the close

coincidence between the two study regions in their percentage of
local material inputs.

Table 7.2
Material inputs derived locally (by value)

Proportion of material inputs derived locally (%)	North West		South East		Total	
	N	%	N	%	N	%
0-24	19	52.8	36	54.5	55	53.9
25-49	8	22.2	13	19.7	21	20.6
50-74	8	22.2	12	18.2	20	19.6
75-100	1	2.8	5	7.6	6	5.9

N = 102

It was anticipated that a different analytical approach to this
question, on the basis of size of plant, might be useful. Indeed,
Gilmour (1974, p341) argues that ' ... it is anticipated that the
external economies of scale available in an agglomeration are
increasingly used as the size of establishment falls'. The responses
on the significance of local material supply linkages were compared
with plant size in Table 7.3, to ascertain the possibility of a
strong relationship between small plant size and importance of local
material supply relationships. Chi square tests performed on this
tabulation yielded a weak significance at the p = 0.02 per cent
level of confidence. An examination of Table 7.3 reveals that
the strength of relationship was reduced by certain very small
plants in the under 20 employees category declaring that local
suppliers were not important.

Table 7.3
Importance of local supply relationships

Plant size (number of employees)	Yes		No	
	N	%*	N	%*
1-19	5	55.6	4	44.4
20-49	15	48.4	16	51.6
50-99	7	31.8	15	68.2
100-199	3	25.0	9	75.0
200-499	5	31.2	11	68.8
500-999	-	-	9	100.0
1,000+over	-	-	3	100.0
Total	35	34.3	67	65.7

chi square = 8.08   p = 0.02

*Proportion of total respondents in any given plant size category

A possible explanation for this weak relationship lies in the
nature of MLH 354 production. A correlation performed later in this
section will show a very poor relationship between plant size and
the number of major product types manufactured. It might normally

be expected that the number of product types manufactured would increase with plant size, but this does not appear to be the case. It was mentioned by certain small establishment executives during the survey that their company was manufacturing (or had on offer) far too many product lines, but since the market was extremely fragmented in requirements and often required tailor-made products, it was frequently difficult to reduce the number of items on offer.

This problem influences linkage interaction with suppliers since, in view of the large numbers of products offered by MLH 354 firms, only a small proportion of the inputs to these generally large product ranges are available locally. Unlike the paint and varnish industry, where Gilmour (1974) found, for this simple form of production, a quite staggering number of inputs, the instruments industry is highly complex. Consequently inputs are frequently of varied specification and type, and spatially dispersed in origin.

Local material input linkages from wholesalers

Further support for the above line of argument evolves from an analysis of interaction with local wholesalers, a specific type of supply linkage. It is generally believed that the use of wholesalers is more prevalent among smaller plants for two major reasons:

1. Small plants are predominantly independent firms. Thus lack of capital resources means that large stocks cannot be held on the premises.

2. Demand for only small quantities of a good inhibits the small manufacturer from negotiating direct supply contracts with large manufacturers.

Hence it might be expected that, whenever possible, small plants will make use of wholesalers. A question was put on what use was made of wholesalers. Of the 102 plant sample 97 (95.1 per cent) establishments acknowledged this form of interaction. Table 7.4 indicates the percentage of total inputs derived from wholesaling sources (by value). This percentage would appear to be generally low, with 43.3 per cent of plants receiving less than 25 per cent of their inputs from wholesalers while a mere 15.5 per cent used this source for over 75 per cent of their inputs.

Table 7.4
Inputs derived from wholesaling sources (by value)

Plant size (number of employees)	Inputs (%)							
	0-24		25-49		50-74		75-100	
	N	%*	N	%*	N	%*	N	%*
1-19	5	55.6	-	-	1	11.1	3	33.3
20-49	11	36.6	8	26.6	6	20.0	5	16.7
50-99	7	33.3	7	33.3	3	14.3	4	19.1
100-199	6	50.0	4	33.3	1	8.3	1	8.3
200-499	7	43.7	6	37.5	1	6.3	2	12.5
500-999	5	71.4	-	-	2	28.6	-	-
1,000+over	1	50.0	1	50.0	-	-	-	-
Total	42	43.3	26	26.8	14	14.4	15	15.5

chi square = 2.78   Not significant at the p = 0.05 per cent level
*Proportion of total respondents in any given plant size category

58

However, to ascertain if there was a tendency for small plants to make greater use of wholesalers, a chi square test was performed on Table 7.4, which compares plant size with wholesaler usage. The poor statistical relationship in Table 7.4 is caused by certain small plants appearing in the under 25 per cent and 50 per cent categories. Certain similarities exist between Table 7.3 and 7.4 in this respect. Apart from the previously stated product complexity problems, and their effects on inputs, a further important factor may be exposed that might help to explain the small plant's lack of interaction with local material suppliers in general and wholesalers in particular.

It has been argued above that small manufacturers would be more likely to make use of local wholesalers if it were feasible. However, Gilmour (1974) found that certain material inputs to particular industries were often limited to one or two national suppliers. Interestingly, little comment has been made in the linkage literature on the relative availability of material supplies and the resultant spatial distribution of linkages. With respect to local linkages in general and wholesalers in particular, an important division of input types must be made between:

1. Standardised (ubiquitous) inputs

2. Specialised inputs.

This division is fundamental to an understanding of the data presented above, and indeed, of input linkages in general. Many of the inputs to MLH 354 plants are of a highly specialised nature. Required tolerances are often so high as to exclude all but the most specialised suppliers. For example, a Manchester plant manufacturing pressure gauges was forced to purchase copper tubing for pressure springs from Switzerland because no British firm could meet the tolerances required, although there were, it should be noted, British firms producing copper tubing of a poorer quality.

Thus the local manufacturing area is frequently unable to supply the inputs required. Moreover, wholesalers generally only stock standardised products (e.g. steel sheet and strip, electronic components). Hence, for specialised inputs, small firms are forced to use manufacturers, since as with MLH 354's own customers, industrial plants within the instruments industry can be fragmented and specialised in their own specifications to suppliers. Further, this absence of a general demand for large quantities of simple standardised components inhibits large companies within the industry, and large suppliers to the industry, from establishing large and exclusive linkage relationships.

Local material input linkages through sub-contracting

Sub-contracting is a further sub-division of linkage interaction which may provide agglomeration economies for industrial firms and is frequently associated with vertically disintergrated industrial forms of production. Any advantages gained from significant interaction on a sub-contract basis would certainly be proof of increased agglomeration economy in the areas where such facilities existed.

Results given in Table 7.5 indicate the extent of sub-contract
activity both in terms of putting out and receiving work. The
majority of establishments are involved in some sub-contract activity;
only nine (8.8 per cent) of plants reporting none. Of the sub-
contracting plants, 54 put out work, 4 received work and 35
experienced both types of flow. The preponderence of putting out
work almost certainly reflects the high technology nature of MLH 354
production. While certain types of routine or dangerous work may
be performed outside MLH 354 plants (e.g. steel frame making, painting,
stove enamelling and asbestos machining), the main type of work that
might be undertaken by instrument firms is highly complex. For
competitive and communications reasons, this form of interaction is
less evident. Communications become more complex when the
sub-contracted item is of a sophisticated specification. Hence,
because MLH 354 products are generally highly complex in specification,
sub-contracting in all but the industry's most technologically simple
products becomes considerably more difficult, and consequently a less
frequent phenomonon (Table 7.5).

Table 7.5
Sub-contracting details

	North West		South East		Total	
	N	%	N	%	N	%
Work put out	12	33.4	42	63.6	54	52.9
Work received	4	11.1	-	-	4	3.9
Both	17	47.2	18	27.3	35	34.3
Neither	3	8.3	6	9.1	9	8.8

N = 102

A further question designed to isolate the strength of sub-contract
bonds between MLH 354 plants and the local area was put to respondents.
This enquiry determined whether respondents thought the local area
possessed advantages in terms of sub-contracting costs and convenience.
Respondents acknowledging these advantages equalled 67 (65.7 per cent)
of the survey sample. Thus a majority indicated that local sub-
contract linkages were important. Other tests on the effects of urban
core locations on the plants claiming sub-contracting advantages
refuted any spatial bias in these establishments. The generally even
distribution of these plants with sub-contracting advantage throughout
the two study regions suggests that the importance of sub-contracting
ties depend more on spatially random factors than upon macro-spatial
agglomerative differences.

Local material input linkages and multi-plant organisations

It is generally accepted that as size of firm increases internalisation
of linkages within its constituent plants should be more feasible
and desirable (Gilmour 1974). Strong linkage internalisation within
the multi plant establishment could prove a distorting influence on
the pattern of linkages for multi plant firms, separating their
linkage behaviour from single plant firms.

It should be generally accepted that if internalisation of inputs
were taking place within a MLH 354 compnay group, then the multi plant

establishments with other local group members might interchange
inputs and outputs. However, only 14 establishments of the 32 multi
plant firm sub-sample with other local group members (within 30 miles)
acknowledged receipt of supplies from other group plants. Moreover,
of these 14 plants, only two establishments received more than
25 per cent of their inputs from local group sources. Hence, there
is a general absence of any strong input linkage effect caused by
internal material linkage flows between plants in multi-plant
organisations.

7.3. NATIONAL MATERIAL INPUT LINKAGE ORIENTATION

A final question, on a macro scale, was put to sample plants asking
if their location caused any problems in securing inputs from
national suppliers (local area excluded). The response was
virtually unanimous. Only one plant admitted to experiencing
problems, this being a plant located in Dover. Clearly, the
peripheral location exacerbated by the inhibiting transport effect
of London for all but London located suppliers, was the major
reason.

The response to this question suggests that the location of
suppliers are so great in number and dispersed that, unlike an
industry with a few major raw material inputs (e.g. steel making),
no single location would be perfect. Hence, any reasonable
transport location is acceptable, explaining the problem displayed
by the Dover plant, the extreme South East having been noted
already as suffering from certain communication difficulties.

7.4. PRODUCTS, OUTPUT LINKAGES AND MLH 354

It should be stated at the outset that it is not expected that
the distribution of output to markets will be found to exert any
great locational influence upon MLH 354 plants. However, this
view was tested, both to prove this assertion and, of equal
importance, to provide useful descriptive information upon the
market characteristics of the instruments industry. For while
location influencing factors are of great interest to researchers
in industrial geography, a study of this type should also include
a degree of description. Analysis in this sub-section begins with
a general appraisal of the size of product ranges and their effect
upon markets.

Major MLH 354 products

It was reasoned that the number of major products offered by a
firm would determine the number and scope of markets available and
thus have some indirect locational effect. Further, as briefly
discussed above, it was hypothesised that plant size would affect
the number of major products on offer in any individual establishment.
Data obtained from a question inquiring as to the number of major
products presented in catalogues were correlated against plant
size. A correlation coefficient of $r = 0.3501$ was obtained. The
weak relationship recorded by the correlation reflects the
considerable number of small establishments with a large number of

products (e.g. one plant employing 55 employees acknowledged 30 main product types on offer to customers). As already emphasised, this tendency for small establishments to produce large numbers of products has a weakening effect on the importance of supply relationships to the MLH 354 plant, but it must also mean that a greater product range reduces the possibility of local market orientation since it is unlikely that all markets could be located in close proximity to the plant.

Local output linkage economies

To ascertain any local market advantages, a question enquired if the loss of local sales through enforced relocation would result in the loss of local market economies. Of the 93 responding plants 80 (86 per cent) establishments indicated that local market economies would not be lost as a result of relocation, thus indicating a strong rejection of the idea of agglomeration economies in respect to markets.

Local output linkages and multi plant organisations

The arguments put forward earlier on the internalising of supply linkages within a company group can also be brought to bear upon outputs from plants since, clearly, the supply linkages of one group plant may be the market linkages of another. Here concern is with any spatial effects that local intra group market linkages may have upon location and, more specifically, upon local agglomeration economies.

Market sales of goods from MLH 354 multi plant establishments to other local group members (within a 30 miles radius) are of low significance. Of the 32 group plants possessing local group members, 13 (40.6 per cent) had no market linkages with other local plants in their group, while a further 18 (56.3 per cent) plants had less than 25 per cent of their output taken by other group plants (most plants dispatched considerably less). On a national level 52 (96.3 per cent) of the 54 multi plant sub-sample dispatched less than 25 per cent of their total output to other group members, indicating the lack of any significant output group interaction at a national level. Thus, group output linkages do not appear to significantly influence the location and organisational structure of MLH 354 survey plants or their markets.

7.5. NATIONAL OUTPUT LINKAGE ORIENTATION

With a view to national markets, a general question enquired if any difficulty was experienced in exploiting distant national markets. A majority of 72 (70.6 per cent) plants within the sample experienced no difficulty. A further question was put to the 30 establishments acknowledging difficulty to attempt to isolate the problems experienced. Table 7.6 indicates that 13 (46.4 per cent) executives asserted that problems in making and maintaining business contacts was the cause of the difficulty, while another 11 respondents considered the problem to result from a combination of excessive transport distance and business contact problems (for indeed, these factors may be complementary). But with only a minority

of plants experiencing difficulties, such problems appear slight
from a locational viewpoint.

Table 7.6
Problems in exploiting distant national
markets

	North West			South East			Total		
	N	% of sub-sample	% of total sample	N	% of sub-sample	% of total sample	N	% of sub-sample	% of total sample
Excessive transport distance	1	9.1	2.8	-	-	-	1	3.5	1.0
Making and maintaining business relationships	6	54.5	16.7	7	41.2	10.6	13	46.5	12.7
Both	4	36.4	11.1	7	41.2	10.6	11	39.3	10.8
Neither	-	-	-	3	17.6	4.5	3	10.7	2.9

N = 28

7.6. OUTPUT LINKAGES AS EXPORTS

Since mid 1971 the governmental Business Statistical Office has
produced figures on the output and exports of MLH 354 on a quarterly
basis. Table 7.7 indicates that, for the four full years available,
exports have averaged a proportion of total production fractionally
below 40 per cent of of the total output of the industry. During
this period exports have kept pace with a sustained growth in
total MLH 354 output.

Table 7.7
MLH 354 exports (£'000's)

	Exports	Total production (by value)	Exports as a percentage of total production
1972	145,128	442,175	32.8
1973	173,865	447,232	38.9
1974	210,670	570,500	36.9
1975	279,996	725,500	38.6

Data from this present study supports the importance of exports
to MLH 354. In Table 7.8 53 establishments (51.9 per cent) sent
between 25 and 75 per cent of their total output in exports to
world markets. All sample plants exported a proportion of their
output. Table 7.9 displays the percentage of total production
exported to other European nations. This question was designed to
ascertain if the South East planning region experienced an advantage
due to its physical proximity to Europe, especially in view of
Britain's entry into the EEC. There is indeed a marginally larger
percentage of output exported from the South East to Europe.

However, any explanation of these data must be based on road-sea
transport since it was frequently mentioned by interviewees in the
North West planning region that the services offered by Manchester's
Ringway Airport compared extremely favourably with Heathrow. Indeed,
some sample plants considered them to be more efficient.

Table 7.8
Proportion of output exported (world)

Percentage of total output (by value)	North West		South East		Total	
	N	%	N	%	N	%
0-24	16	44.4	22	33.3	38	37.2
25-49	10	27.8	17	25.8	27	26.5
50-74	6	16.7	20	30.3	26	25.5
75-100	4	11.1	7	10.6	11	10.8

N = 102

Table 7.9
Proportion of output exported (Europe)

Percentage of total output (by value)	North West		South East		Total	
	N	%	N	%	N	%
0-24	29	80.5	45	69.2	74	73.3
25-49	6	16.7	14	21.5	20	19.8
50-74	1	2.8	6	9.2	7	6.9
75-100	-	-	-	-	-	-

N = 101

7.7. CONCLUSION

The agglomerative effect of inputs and outputs on MLH 354 location
has been low. It has been argued that this weak effect of linkages
is mainly due to the high technology nature of MLH 354 production
which ensures that both inputs to, and outputs from, MLH 354 plants
are diverse in specifcation and origin. Constant product change
and the wide range of products offered by all sizes of MLH 354
establishments result in fragmented input and output linkage patterns
which generally tend to negate the predominance of any particular
suppliers or customers.

8 Labour

8.1. INTRODUCTION

When considering the effects of labour on the location of industrial
production, it must be remembered that the establishment of a new
firm is relatively rare. The majority of new production locations
arise from the movement of an existing business in total, or from
the opening of a branch plant of an existing company. In these
instances, where location decision makers are not undertaking
the location decision with a 'blank sheet of paper', the consideration
of an existing labour force has an important restraining influence
upon company strategy. Critically with the total relocation, and
less so in the case of the branch plant establishment, the
relocating firm will seek to persuade key personnel to move with
the relocated production. In this situation, the influence of
labour on location may be stronger in the location of origin than
in the area of the new site.

The extent to which a relocating firm will be restricted in its
mobility by the existing labour force will be largely determined
by the numbers of key workers required to move with a proposed
relocation. Clearly, high technology industries will require a larger
proportion of their workforce to move with the establishment. Such
workers are essential both for their own productive effort and for
their capacity as trainers of skilled labour in the new location.
Moreover, if the technology of the relocating firm is complex there
will be a reduced likelihood of suitable workers being available in
the area of the chosen relocation. But for the executives of any
company, irrespective of the numbers of workers required to move
during a relocation, decisions will be taken in the knowledge that
not all key personnel will be retained during movement and that a
degree of inefficiency in the new location will inevitably ensue.
The concept of 'bounded rationality' is applicable here (Simon, 1947),
in that the costs and benefits of a relocation cannot be accurately
pre-determined. Understandably, this reality frequently results in
a tendency to indefinitely postpone a relocation decision.

Ignoring problems of labour mobility, the traditional view of many
economists, that the labour market operates on a supply and demand
basis, and will hence find its own spatial equilbrium, is clearly
put by Gitlow (1954, p62) when he argues 'Labour reacts to wage
differentials by moving to jobs offering the most favourable terms
and conditions'. This view of workers' attitudes neglects the
strong behavioural factors that restrict the mobility of employees.
The consideration of wage levels is but one of the total spectrum
of factors which act upon potentially mobile workers and include
housing, schools and family ties. The proposition that labour is,
in current conditions in Britain, immobile, would appear more
intuitively logical and is further supported by the empirical and

theoretical observations of other researchers (Luttrell 1962, Clegg 1965).

Although the stimulus for relocation can frequently be traced to forces external to the firm (e.g. expiry of lease, site claimed for redevelopment), examples exist where the attractions of an abundant or cheap labour supply have acted as a positive location factor. Lloyd and Dicken (1972) assert that, for both the USA and Britain, spatial differences in wage levels do exist despite union activity aimed towards regional parity in recent years. Companies operating production methods which require mainly unskilled labour, or establishing a branch plant designed to specialise in low skill areas of company operations, may be attracted to regions of low cost unskilled labour.

Indeed, for certain industries, the national and international locations of production have been radically affected. Vyver (1951) noted that the most important cause of the decline of the New England textile industry and its subsequent growth in the southern states was the lower wage levels of the south. On an international scale, Riley (1973) attributes the growth of textile manufacture in Japan, Hong Kong and Portugal, at the expense of the traditional producing areas of Western Europe, to the lower wage levels of these countries. Cost advantages afforded by low regional wage levels are most applicable to firms employing large numbers of semi-skilled and unskilled workers. These types of workers are easily adapted to perform simple production operations and, hence, productivity can be rapidly increased in the new plant. Further, few key workers are required to establish the new production plant.

However, relocating firms with only moderate skill requirements may find the scarcity of suitable labour in a new location a serious problem. In their study of the motor industry, Goodman and Samuel (1966) discovered that serious difficulties were experienced by their case study firm in obtaining a suitable number of skilled and semi-skilled operatives in the firm's new location. The authors further emphasised that this shortage was surprising since it occurred in a development area of above average national unemployment. Consequently, it may be observed that a form of production technologically more sophisticated than motor vehicle assembly might experience more serious skilled labour supply difficulties after relocation if a considerable proportion of the existing staff could not be persuaded to move to the new site. This assertion has obvious relevance to MLH 354 and the present study and finds support from the case studies reported in Chapter 10.

All these comments on the effects of labour on location will be relevant to the following analysis. In particular, the comments on the importance of the behaviour of existing workers to the location of industry are paramount to an understanding of the effects of labour on the location of MLH 354 production. The analysis begins with an indication of the areas of Britain where MLH 354 employment is important.

8.2. THE DISTRIBUTION OF MLH 354 EMPLOYMENT

The national distribution

The location quotient map (Figure 8.1) has been constructed from 1971
Census of Population industrial data at the local authority level
for the whole of Britain. Fortunately the comprehensive coverage of
MLH 354 employment figures for all local authorities in Britain was
kindly made available by the London School of Economics' Urban Change
Project. Only partial local authority coverage is generally
available from published sources. This location quotient map gives
the reader a general impression of the major specialist areas of
MLH 354 production. Each dot represents a local authority where
MLH 354 production warrants a location quotient greater than unity,
thereby indicating some degree of instrument industry specialisation.

However, this map is best viewed generally, grouping dots into
wide areas of specialisation rather than considering them individually,
since the method of calculating location quotients may occasionally
yield high location quotient values in areas where the total working
population is low. In such instances, there is specialisation, but
within only a small total working population. This phenomenon may
occur in rural areas where a government or private MLH 354 factory
dominates the local employment structure. However, in instances
where groups of dots are observable, both specialisation and general
employment importance may be assumed.

If the location quotient map is analysed in conjunction with the
distribution of MLH 354 employment at the planning region level
(Table 8.1), both sources indicate the importance of the South East
and North West planning regions as the major centres of instrument
industry production (52.5 per cent and 15.7 per cent of national
employment respectively). Scotland appears as a poor third with
8.7 per cent of the national MLH 354 workforce with an area of

Table 8.1
Regional distribution of MLH 354 employment (1971)

Standard planning region	Thousands	Proportion of MLH 354 UK employment
North	2.3	1.9
Yorks & Humberside	3.2	2.6
East Midlands	3.4	2.8
East Anglia	4.2	3.5
South East	62.9	52.5
South West	7.7	6.4
West Midlands	5.0	4.2
North West	18.8	15.7
Wales	1.9	1.5
Scotland	10.3	8.7

specialisation around Edinburgh (Figure 8.1). The South West,
fourth in importance in Table 8.1 (6.4 per cent of national employment),
is based on an area of specialisation in the Gloucester/Cheltenham
district. The dominance of the two planning regions chosen for the

67

(Each dot equals one Local Authority)

Location Quotient Score

o : 1 to 4·9

● : 5 and over

Miles

0   60

Figure 8.1   Location quotient map of MLH 354 employment in Britain

study is abundantly clear; these regions combine to account for over 68 per cent of total MLH 354 production. Detailed analysis of MLH 354 employment in these planning regions now follows.

8.3. SUB-REGIONAL ANALYSIS OF EMPLOYMENT IN THE NORTH WEST AND SOUTH EAST PLANNING REGIONS

The data presented in map form in Figures 8.2 to 8.5 are again based on 1971 industrial census data (10 per cent sample). Both in the North West and South East, the local authority boundaries indicated are those current in 1971 since the data pertained to these areas and not to the new divisions. This difference should not generally affect the general impression of MLH 354 distribution afforded by the data. However, in the interests of conformity, the 1971 planning region boundaries have been amended to conform to the current post-1974 areas.

For each planning region a more finely calibrated location quotient map, indicating actual local authority boundaries, has been constructed. These maps are supported by further employment density maps of the two major built up areas of the planning regions (i.e. the Greater Manchester and Greater London conurbations). These additional maps are necessary since the location quotient method, while clearly indicating specialisation, tends to under-stress important MLH 354 production areas when the total working population is very high. Hence, these labour intensity maps will indicate certain areas which do not appear strongly on the location quotient maps because of a large total workforce, but which nevertheless are important to MLH 354 production.

The North West

The regional location quotient map for the North West (Figure 8.2) is clearly dominated by the areas of specialisation within the Manchester conurbation. With the exception of Skelmersdale and Runcorn, the map is dominated by local authorities in, or fringing, Manchester. The large area of MLH 354 specialisation south of Manchester (Macclesfield Rural District) has gained a significant location quotient value through its low total working population and the proximity of its most northern margins to the southern suburbs of the Manchester conurbation. New government sponsored estates have provided MLH 354 employment in Skelmersdale and Runcorn and lie behind the significant location quotient values obtained for these local authorities. Indeed, both these industrial developments produced a plant for the present MLH 354 survey sample.

The remaining areas in Figure 8.2 recording significant location quotient values are confined to the Manchester conurbation. Significantly, three distinct and separate districts may be isolated within the Manchester urban area. The first district is in the north west of the conurbation, including the Oldham, Royton, Farnworth, Audenshaw and Denton local authorities. (See Figure 8.3 for identification of these local authorities). This district is centred on the two large Ferranti factories at Moston and Hollingwood which have, since the turn of the century, provided a basis for instrument industry skills in an area which has declined environmentally since

69

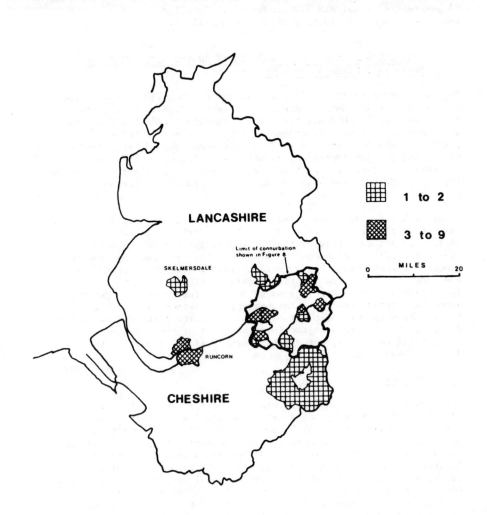

Figure 8.2 Location quotient map of the North West planning region

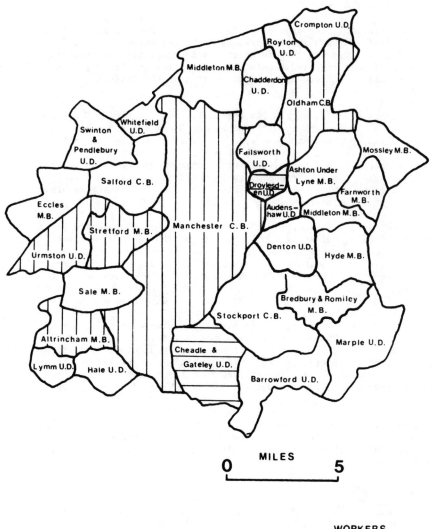

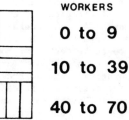

WORKERS

0 to 9

10 to 39

40 to 70

Figure 8.3   MLH 354 employment in the Greater Manchester conurbation
(1971 boundaries)

the first world war.

The second district exposed by location quotient map in Figure 8.3
is the Trafford Park area comprising the local authorities of
Stretford and Urmston. Again this area is characterised by ageing
industrial buildings and housing, being centred on the important
AEI Scientific Instrument plant at Urmston on the Trafford Park
Estate.

The final district of MLH 354 specialisation within the Manchester
conurbation is that of the Altrincham and Cheadle and Gately local
authorities on the south west fringe of the built up area. Although
dominated by the large Edwardian plants of the Record Electrical
and Budenberg Gauge companies at Altrincham, the area is environmentally
more pleasing than the two previously mentioned districts, with a
proportion of smaller new plants attracted by the pleasant suburban
character of the district.

The local authority areas of the Manchester conurbation are shown
in Figure 8.3, indicating the number of MLH 354 workers employed
in each local authority area (10 per cent survey). As might be
generally expected, the three districts isolated above in Figure 8.2
are detectable in Figure 8.3. The major difference between these
two Figures, where they deal with the Manchester conurbation, is the
appearance of Manchester County Borough as a significant area for
MLH 354 employment, in Figure 8.3. However, it is only possible to
speculate on the significance of such a large area to MLH 354
employment. On the one hand, there can be little doubt that the
borough's huge total employment figure destroyed any possibility of
a significant location quotient value; while conversely, the large
size of the area may well have produced a larger MLH 354 employment
figure than many districts within the borough would have achieved
alone.

However, with minor exceptions, the employment data reflects the
location quotient material for the North West in supporting the
importance of MLH 354 production districts at Oldham, Trafford Park
and Altrincham.

The South East

The detailed location quotient map of the South East planning region
has, as with the North West, been modified where possible to suit
new planning region and county boundaries. Beginning the analysis
of Figure 8.4 at a general level it is at once possible to note
a broad corridor of MLH 354 specialisation which extends from the
south coast between Portsmouth and Eastbourne northwards through
Greater London and East Berkshire to the planning region boundary,
incorporating parts of Buckinghamshire, Bedfordshire and Hertfordshire.
On closer inspection it can be seen that there are gaps in this
corridor in North West Sussex, the southern part of Surrey, North
Buckinghamshire and North West Bedfordshire.

These gaps in MLH 354 specialisation emphasise a number of areas
of general MLH 354 importance. Beginning on the South Coast, and
moving northwards, a coastal belt between Eastbourne in the east
and Portsmouth in the west is detectable, especially in the Brighton

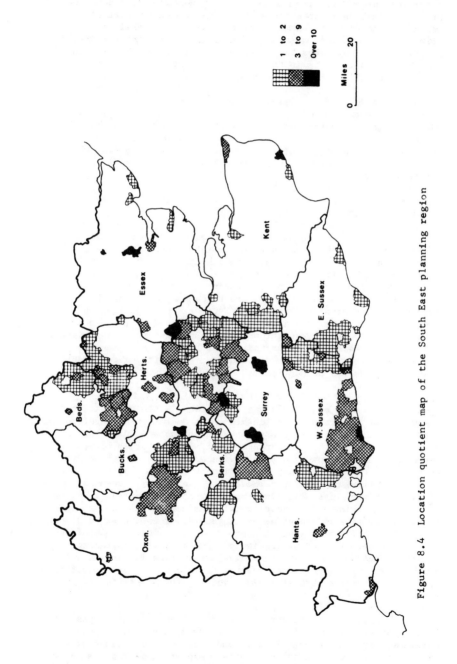

Figure 8.4 Location quotient map of the South East planning region

and Hove district. This environmentally pleasing zone may well have become important for MLH 354 production due to the movement of industrial production from London. Moving northwards, a small area of specialisation is detectable in the north western part of Hampshire and the eastern margins of Surrey in the Basingstoke, Farnborough, Camberley district. The post war migration of MLH 354 plants from London, plus the presence of various government linked research establishments in the Farnborough area may well explain much of the rationale for this concentration.

Greater London and its immediate environs provide the major general concentration of MLH 354 specialisation in the planning region. Within Greater London itself, Enfield and Barnet in the north west, and Kingston, Merton, Croydon and Lewisham in the south west and south form a continuous arc of specialisation from the north through the west to the south. Immediately outside the Greater London boundary, Watford, St. Albans and Elstree appear with location quotients in the three to nine range, while in the north east, south and south west, Chigwell, Reigate and New Windsor respectively score over ten.

To the north west of London, on the Oxfordshire-Buckinghamshire borders, a moderate zone of specialisation extends from Beaconsfield (location quotient of over ten), through High Wycombe, to Bullingdon Rural District in the south east of Oxfordshire. The post war movement of firms from the north western areas of London (e.g. Park Royal) along the line of the A40 trunk road may explain the importance of Beaconsfield and High Wycombe, while Bullingdon Rural District in Oxfordshire must have benefited from the nearby presence of several government research establishments (e.g. Harwell and Culham). Moreover, since this Rural District fringes on Oxford's northern, eastern and southern city limits, a degree of instrument industry production may be stimulated by university patronage.

One further zone of MLH 354 specialisation is clearly evident in the north of the planning region along the Bedfordshire-Herdfordshire borders. This area stretches from Leighton Buzzard in the south west, continuing in an arc through Luton, Welwyn Garden City, Stevenage and Letchworth to Biggleswade and Royston in the north east. This area offers many attractions to the MLH 354 firm which is either forced to move or relocates to the positive advantages of an outer south east location from a Greater London site. Proximity to London is a great advantage since it allows both the personal contacts of individual employees and the linkage relationships of the firm to be maintained if required. The availability of new housing for workers and modern factory premises are additional advantages to this already attractive area. Finally, unlike the south coast zone discussed above, the M1 motorway offers an efficient connection to the rest of Britain, avoiding the congestion of London.

As with the data on the North West, for the most densely populated area of the South East (i.e. Greater London), instrument industry employment is plotted for all the London boroughs in Figure 8.5. This will clarify the location quotient map where it applies to the boroughs in which a large total employment figure has obscured

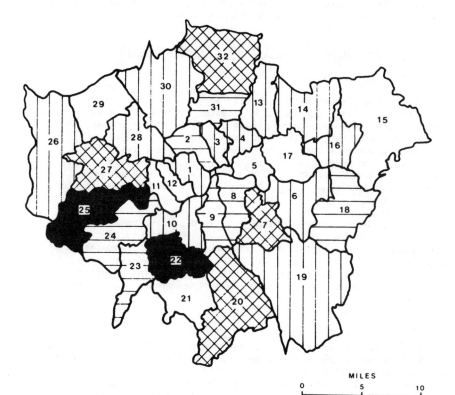

MILES

0   5   10

LONDON BOROUGHS

1	Westminster	17	Newham
2	Camden	18	Bexley
3	Islington	19	Bromley
4	Hackney	20	Croydon
5	Tower Hamlets	21	Sutton
6	Greenwich	22	Merton
7	Lewisham	23	Kingston
8	Southwark	24	Richmond
9	Lambeth	25	Hounslow
10	Wandsworth	26	Hillingdon
11	Hammersmith	27	Ealing
12	Kensington & Chelsea	28	Brent
13	Waltham Forest	29	Harrow
14	Redbridge	30	Barnet
15	Havering	31	Haringey
16	Barking	32	Enfield

0 – 19

20 – 49

50 – 139

140 – 174

175 – 250

Figure 8.5   MLH 354 employment in the London Boroughs

the labour importance of MLH 354. In fact the employment intensity
map in Figure 8.5 closely resembles the arc of MLH 354 specialisation
within the Greater London area noted from Figure 8.4.

8.4. A SUMMARY OF EMPLOYMENT IN THE TWO PLANNING REGIONS

The North West

The impression created by Figure 8.2 is generally static in the
sense that the districts in the Manchester conurbation to emerge as
specialist MLH 354 zones were predominantly well established.
Certainly the Oldham and Trafford Park districts are more notable
for their industrial decline than modern industrial expansion.
Conversely, the Altrincham district of south west Manchester was
different in that a traditional MLH 354 base has been augmented by
an attractive environment for the development of new firms in the
area.

Moreover, the relatively static general distribution of MLH 354
employment in the North West has no doubt been influenced by less
official pressure regarding planning permission in urban areas when
compared with the South East. Further, abundant factory space
in existing industrial areas, provided by the declining cotton
industry, reduces the need for long distance movement from existing
urban locations.

The South East

The South East planning region's distribution of MLH 354 employment,
unlike that of the North West, must be viewed in the context of the
post war distribution of industry policies and the very real costs
of congestion that London has produced during the past 30 years.
Combining the maps of Figures 8.4 and 8.5 it may be recalled that
a general crescent of MLH 354 employment concentration exists,
ranging from Enfield in the north, through Brent, Ealing, Hounslow,
Kingston and Merton, to Croydon and Lewisham in the South.

But, more interestingly, a further arc of MLH 354 specialisation
is evident in Figure 8.5, if the outer south eastern districts of
specialisation isolated above are combined on a general level.
Following the south coast zone centred on Brighton north westwards
through the Basingstoke, Farnborough, Camberley area, northward
through the Bullingdon, High Wycombe, Beaconsfield district, and then
north eastward to the Luton, Welwyn Garden City, Stevenage, Biggleswade,
Royston area, a general crescent of MLH 354 specialisation may be
observed at a distance of between approximately 25 and 50 miles from
central London.

Although it is accepted that this crescent is highly generalised,
it runs through a sector of a circle based on London's centre from
north through west to south, which replicates at a larger scale and
on an increased radius the above mentioned Greater London crescent
extending from Enfield to Lewisham. Moreover, it is notable that an
area of weak MLH 354 specialisation on the eastern side of Greater
London is mirrored by a larger area of low instrument industry
specialisation in the counties of Kent, Essex and the Northern

part of East Sussex.

Thus it may be tentatively suggested that the outer south eastern crescent exposed above may have been formatively influenced by the location of existing major areas of instrument industry production in Greater London. It may be that firms relocating from central London prefer to move to outer south eastern locations by relocating in the direction of lines drawn from the centre of London through their existing plant rather than by crossing London's built up area.

8.5. THE OCCUPATIONAL STRUCTURE OF THE MLH 354 WORKFORCE

Before proceeding with the analysis of the occupational structure of MLH 354, there follows below a brief explanation of the employment definitions used in the questionnaire survey. These were:

1. Highly skilled technical/managerial. Several criteria were used to define this worker, including a position of seniority, a professional qualification, a degree or an equivalent academic attainment. This group included all senior administrators not involved physically in the production process, but not test engineers working directly on the production line.

2. Skilled. This category was more easily defined and included qualified tradesmen who had completed an officially recognised apprenticeship or course to fit them for skilled work on the shop floor.

3. Semi-skilled. The semi-skilled group of workers was more difficult to define precisely. It is frequently difficult to draw a line between an unskilled labourer with a certain degree of acquired skill and a truly semi-skilled operative. However, after consultation with MLH 354 executives during initial pilot interviews, it was decided to define a semi-skilled worker as an operative who required between two and six weeks initial training to perform the task concerned but did not obtain any skill qualification for the abilities acquired.

The semi-skilled category is important since it covers the important contribution made by most female employees to MLH 354 production. These women, who are predominantly housewives with family commitments have never been in a position to undergo an apprenticeship or training course. Hence, though frequently full time employees, the task of such women is to perform semi-skilled light mechanical assembly or electrical wiring tasks on the shop floor. These jobs, although frequently highly skilled in terms of the speed with which they may be performed, do not require intensive training. Hence it was agreed with MLH 354 executives that the six weeks maximum training rule would adequately incorporate this group of workers. The semi-skilled category within MLH 354 is mainly composed of women and junior male trainees in the course of obtaining skilled status.

4. Unskilled. This final category was the most easily defined. The criterion used was 'no skills necessary to perform task'.

It was necessary to test certain hypotheses that have been applied
to high technology and high value added industry and thus, indirectly,
to MLH 354. Central to any assertion on the labour requirements of
industries making technically sophisticated products is the belief
that very few unskilled workers would be required by such firms.
Thus members of the MLH 354 study sample were asked to estimate the
percentage of their workforce which could be classified as unskilled.
As might be expected 97 (95.1 per cent of the respondent plants)
claimed that less than 25 per cent of their workforce were unskilled.

Of the remaining five plants, three were included in the 25 per cent
to 49 per cent size range, while the remaining two plants responded
in the 50 per cent to 74 per cent category. On further inspection,
four of these five plants using over 25 per cent unskilled labour
were large by general sample standards (i.e. 950, 750, 300 and
500 employees respectively) and were engaged in forms of instrument
making which involved a great deal of general engineering work,
using technology which was comparatively well established and
stable (e.g. steam pressure gauges and electricity meter production).
Nevertheless, despite these exceptions, unskilled labour would
appear to be unimportant to MLH 354 production. It may be subsequently
deduced therefore that semi-skilled and skilled workers are of great
importance to MLH 354 production.

8.6. FEMALE WORKERS: THEIR IMPORTANCE TO MLH 354 PRODUCTION

It has been generally acknowledged for many years that certain
industrial operations, especially those concerned with electronic
assembly, are performed well by female workers, due to their high
levels of patience and manual dexterity. Since certain aspects of
instrument making involves complex electronic assembly, it was
considered relevant to ascertain the importance of female workers
in the shop floor activities of MLH 354 establishments (female
office staff were excluded from the present analysis).

Respondents were asked to estimate, for unskilled and semi-skilled
manual workers, the percentage of female workers contained within
these categories in their plants. Table 8.2 indicates that, for
both the North West and South East, approximately 50 per cent of
the survey sample reported that over 25 per cent of their unskilled
and semi-skilled workforce were women. Since it has been established
in the previous sub-section that unskilled workers are of little
importance to MLH 354, the majority of these women must be semi-skilled.

Table 8.2
Female workers as a percentage of unskilled and semi-skilled
shop floor workforce

Percentage female workers	North West		South East		Total	
	N	%	N	%	N	%
0-24	18	50.0	30	45.4	48	47.1
25-49	5	13.9	6	9.1	11	10.8
50-74	5	13.9	23	34.9	28	27.5
75-100	8	22.2	7	10.6	15	14.7

It was considered that size of plant might be acting as a determinant of the percentage of female workers employed in unskilled and semi-skilled shop floor worker categories. This assertion would be valid if larger plants, through the introduction of large scale standardised production methods, were employing women as unskilled and semi-skilled machine mainders. The chi square test performed on Table 8.3 yielded no significance at the $p = 0.05$ per cent level, indicating no relationship between size of plant and the propensity to employ unskilled and semi-skilled female workers.

Table 8.3
Proportion of female workers against size of plant

Plant size (number of employees)	Female workers (%)							
	0-24		25-49		50-74		75-100	
	N	%*	N	%*	N	%*	N	%*
1-19	4	44.5	-	-	2	22.2	3	33.3
20-49	17	54.8	2	6.5	7	22.6	5	16.1
50-99	12	54.5	4	18.2	5	22.7	1	4.6
100-199	4	33.3	2	16.7	5	41.7	1	8.3
200-499	6	37.5	2	12.5	7	43.7	1	6.3
500-999	4	44.5	1	11.1	1	11.1	3	33.3
1000+over	1	33.3	-	-	1	33.3	1	33.3
Total	48	47.1	11	10.8	28	27.4	15	14.7

chi square 1.37   Not significant at the $p = 0.05$ per cent level
* Proportion of total respondents in any given size category

The apparently random distribution of MLH 354 female shop floor workers in plants throughout the instruments industry might more reasonably be explained by differences in the technology which exists between plants. Although no means of testing this hypothesis from existing survey data exists, the extent of electronic technology within a firm's instrument making operations may well be highly correlated with the extent to which female workers are utilised. Observations made in the factories during interviews strongly suggest that the majority of MLH 354 semi skilled women workers were employed as 'wire-women'.

This is work in which the soldering of the electronic components of instruments is undertaken by semi-skilled personnel using a step-by-step schedule, previously designed by a skilled engineer. Wire women must constitute a high proportion of the total shop floor workforce within MLH 354. However, the number of women employed in the making of electronic parts for instruments does not depend merely upon the electronic contribution made to any given product. Strategic decisions made by management will determine if a particular item is produced within the factory or sub-contracted out to another specialised firm. This decision will in turn affect the numbers of women required to perform wiring tasks. (Printed circuit boards are a good example of a component manufactured by certain instrument firms while sub-contracted out by others). Nevertheless, it is clear that female semi-skilled labour is important to a significant proportion of the MLH 354 survey sample plants (Table 8.2). It is further thought that the majority of these women are employed by plants with a strong electronic technological bias.

8.7. INDIRECT LABOUR AND MLH 354 PRODUCTION

Part of the analysis of this sub-section has been previously presented in Chapter 4 on Organisation, where the importance of research and development staff to MLH 354 was considered (pp 24-27). Tests showed that, although the number of research workers employed in MLH 354 establishments increased significantly with plant size, the <u>percentage</u> of the total workforce employed in research and development did not increase with the size of the establishment. It was considered that, due to the central importance of research and development to MLH 354 production, small plants were as keen as their larger counterparts to invest manpower in the pursuit of new and improved products.

However, research workers, although important to MLH 354, are only part of the total indirect labour force within the industry. But it might be expected that research workers would offer the most logical explanation for any high proportion of indirect labour within MLH 354, since other indirect workers (e.g. executive staff, book-keepers and secretaries) are required in approximately the same numbers throughout all forms of industrial production.

The results of a question requiring an indication of the percentage of the sample plants' workforces engaged in indirect labour occupations are given in Table 8.4. The assertion that MLH 354 possesses a high level of indirect workers is supported by the observation that almost half (40.2 per cent) of respondents acknowledged between 50 per cent and 74 per cent of their workforce as indirect, with only 28.4 per cent of plants claiming less than 25 per cent of their workforce not employed in direct productive effort.

Size of plant might be a general determinant of the percentage of workers not directly employed on the shop floor in industrial plants. It may be noted from Table 8.5 that for certain randomly

Table 8.4

Proportion of indirect labour force against size of plant

Plant size (number of employees)	Indirect workers (%)							
	0-24		25-49		50-74		75-100	
	N	%*	N	%*	N	%*	N	%*
1-19	5	55.6	2	22.2	2	22.2	-	-
20-49	12	38.7	11	35.5	7	22.6	1	3.2
50-99	7	31.8	6	27.3	8	36.4	1	4.5
100-199	2	16.7	5	41.7	5	41.7	-	-
200-499	1	6.2	3	18.8	12	75.0	-	-
500-999	1	11.1	2	22.2	6	66.7	-	-
1000+over	1	33.3	-	-	1	33.3	1	33.3
Total	29	28.4	29	28.4	41	40.2	3	2.9

chi square 14.55   Significant at the p = 0.001 per cent level
* Proportion of total respondents in any given size category

selected industries of diverse technological type (including MLH 354), in every instance the percentage of indirect workers increases with

the size of plant. Thus it may be accepted that there is a general
tendency for the percentages of indirect labour to increase in any
industrial sector with an increase in plant size. Moreover, a chi
square test on the sample responses to the indirect labour question,
comparing the level of indirect labour with plant size, was highly
significant at the $p = 0.001$ per cent level (Table 8.4).

This test of the survey sample supports the Census of Production
evidence given in Table 8.5. However, since it has been shown
in Chapter 4 on Organisation that the proportion of research workers,
as a percentage of the MLH 354 employment totals, does not generally
increase with plant size, the observed growth in the percentage of
indirect workers with size for MLH 354 plants must be largely due to
the greater bureaucracy which results from the increased complexity
of organisation that accompanies larger plant size.

Table 8.5
Percentage change in indirect workers in the smallest and largest
size categories for a range of MLH types

| Industrial type | Size categories | | Percentage change |
	Smallest %*	Largest %*	
MLH 354	35.6	45.0	+ 9.4
Radio, radar and electronic capital goods	41.7	56.8	+ 15.1
Rubber	21.5	30.5	+ 9.0
Soap and detergents	35.1	52.0	+ 16.9
Wheeled tractors manufacturing	13.9	26.4	+ 12.5

Census of Production 1972
* Proportion of indirent workers

The inability to use the percentage of research workers as a means
of explaining the proportionate increase of indirect labour with
MLH 354 plant size does not detract from the general importance of
this group of workers to the instruments industry. Indeed, Table 8.6
indicates that scientific instruments, computer and radio, radar and
electronic capital goods industrial sectors employ consistently
higher proportions of indirect workers (i.e. 39.7, 78.7 and 42.9
per cent respectively) than are evidenced by other high value added
industries. These other industries with a lower indirect labour
proportion in their workforces are jewellery and precious metals and
musical instrument making (i.e. 24.9 and 22.3 per cent respectively).
Both sets of High Value Added data were taken from the 1972 Census of
Production. (In order to avoid distortions which might have occurred
because of the variable size structure of the different industries
concerned, the 100 to 199 employment size category was used
throughout).

It is significant to note that these two industries with low
proportions of indirect labour are both forms of production where
technology is highly stabilised and where research and development
is minimal. The difference in the amount of research and development
must largely explain the differences in the proportions of indirect

81

labour evidenced between the two industrial groups of high value adding industries, since as previously mentioned, requirements for other indirect workers would be approximately the same for any organisation of similar size.

Table 8.6
Indirect workers as a percentage of total employment for a range of high value added MLH types

Industrial type	Percentage of indirect workers (100-199 size category)
MLH 354	39.7
Computers	78.7
Radio, radar and electronic capital goods	42.9
Jewellery and precious metals	24.9
Musical instrument making	22.3

Census of Production 1972

Having considered certain quantitative aspects of the MLH 354 labour force, the concern of this section is now directed towards views expressed within the industry itself on the spatial variations in instrument industry labour supply and quality.

8.8. SPATIAL VARIATIONS IN MLH 354 LABOUR SKILLS

Since the majority of the study sample plants were established, and the remainder were short distance relocations, questions on the orientation of MLH 354 plants towards inter-regional supplies of labour were not relevant. However, as a means of ascertaining whether there is a spatial variation in labour quality, established and relocated plants were asked to assess subjectively the standard of local labour skills. Any spatial bias in preferences might reflect the agglomeration advantages of a rich and varied local labour supply asserted to be important by Gilmour (1974).

A question enquiring if the respondent's location benefited from specialised local labour skills was put to interviewees. Table 8.7 indicates the surprisingly low affirmative response rate of 32 (31.4 per cent) plants. Since the North West and South East planning regions have been shown to be the most concentrated areas of MLH 354 employment, it might reasonably have been expected that a more favourable set of evaluations would have been produced by respondents.

Table 8.7
Respondents claiming local labour skill advantages

	North West		South East		Total	
	N	%	N	%	N	%
Local labour skill advantage	9	25.0	23	34.9	32	31.4
No local labour skill advantage	27	75.0	43	65.1	70	68.6

However, it must be noted that all questionnaire responses are to
some extent subjective, especially when the responses are qualitative.
Indeed, in many cases observed by the interviewer, interviewees, due
to the established nature of their business, had no means of comparing
their local labour markets with other locales. Hence, since employable
labour for MLH 354 production is certain to be scarce, even in the
best MLH 354 employment areas, it is not surprising that a respondent
with only a limited knowledge of comparative spatial differences in
labour quality might be pessimistic towards his own local labour pool.
The importance of perception in interviewees' evaluations of MLH 354
labour factors will be examined below.

Table 8.8 indicates that any urban agglomerative bias of MLH 354
plants claiming a good local labour environment is weak. The percentage
of establishments acknowledging good labour skill environments
located in Zone 1 (i.e. the area enclosed by the circumference of
a 15 mile radius circle based on the centres of London and Manchester),
for both the North West and South East planning regions were compared
with the total sample percentages for this central zone. In keeping
with previous analysis Zone 2 constituted the remaining area from
the edge of Zone 1 to the planning region boundary.

Table 8.8
Distribution of respondents claiming local labour skill advantages

	North West						South East					
	Zone 1		Zone 2		Total		Zone 1		Zone 2		Total	
	N	%	N	%	N	%	N	%	N	%	N	%
Respondents claiming local labour skill advantages	6	66.6	3	33.3	9	100	10	43.5	13	56.5	23	100
Survey plants in zone	22	61.1	14	38.9	36	100	25	37.9	41	62.1	66	100

N = 32

A small percentage bias was detectable for both the North West and
South East planning regions among plants claiming local labour
advantages in favour of Zone 1 (i.e. 5.5 and 5.6 respectively).
However, since the plants acknowledging a good local labour
environment were in the minority (32 plants), this marginal bias
in favour of the urban Zone 1 cannot be accepted as proof of labour
advantage stemming from agglomeration. This rejection is enhanced
by the greater number of establishments in Zone 1, for both the
North West and South East planning regions who did not acknowledge
local labour skill advantages. But any assertions stemming from
this local labour skills question must be seriously qualified by the
noted subjectivity of the above responses.

8.9. LOCAL LABOUR SHORTAGES

Luttrell (1962) and Townroe (1971) have observed through their
own empirical work that problems experienced over the scarcity of
suitable labour can provide a major incentive towards relocation.

But as previously mentioned an executive's knowledge of potential
new and improved locations from a labour viewpoint may be poor, thus
inhibiting any positive moves towards a relocation solution to a
manpower shortage problem. Further, as will be indicated in
the chapter on relocation (Chapter 10), the potential loss of key
workers may cancel out any advantage gained from more abundant labour
supplies in a new location. Nevertheless, the problems experienced
in obtaining labour are worthy of consideration since a more
significant measure of the quality of the local labour market is
facilitated.

Table 8.9 indicates the results of a question enquiring if there
was a problem in obtaining a particular type of local labour skill.
The most immediately apparent factor to emerge from the table is
the considerable difference in response patterns produced by the
two planning regions with regard to 'no labour problems'. The
North West planning region exceeded the South Eastern establishments
by a ratio of almost two to one in this category (41.7 per cent and
24.4 per cent respectively). This result is of particular interest
since it conflicts with many of the negative assertions made by
certain executives in the North West when asked to assess the best
region for MLH 354 labour in the following sub-section.

Table 8.9
Local labour supply problems by region

Type of labour	North West N	North West %	South East N	South East %	Total N	Total %
Skilled	11	30.6	11	16.7	22	21.6
Unskilled	-	-	-	-	-	-
Highly skilled technical managerial	3	8.3	3	4.5	6	5.9
Skilled/ unskilled	2	5.5	3	4.5	5	4.9
Highly skilled technical managerial/ skilled	4	11.1	10	15.1	14	13.7
Highly skilled technical managerial/ unskilled	-	-	-	-	-	-
All types a problem	1	2.8	23	34.9	24	23.5
No labour problems	15	41.7	16	24.2	31	30.4

N = 102

Table 8.10 has been constructed to simplify the data in Table 8.9,
which is somewhat unclear in that the 'all labour types a problem'
category applies to all the three labour types. It becomes clear
that, for all labour types, the plants in the South East planning
region experience greater difficulty with regard to the acquisition of

labour than do the plants of the North West, a factor which is not readily apparent from Table 8.9. These problems of labour supply, combined with the responses on 'no labour problems' suggest strongly that South Eastern plants experience far greater difficulty than their North Western counterparts in obtaining suitable labour.

Table 8.10
Local labour supply problems: Table 8.9 reconstructed*

Type of labour	North West N	%	South East N	%	Total N	%
Skilled	18	50.0	47	71.2	65	63.7
Unskilled	3	8.3	26	39.4	29	28.4
Highly skilled technical managerial	7	19.4	36	54.5	43	42.2

* Percentages total more than 100 per cent due to certain plants appearing in more than one category

8.10. PERCEIVED REGIONAL VARIATIONS IN LABOUR QUALITY

The problems of subjectivity and partial knowledge on the part of the interviewee, and their possible distortive effect on results, have been discussed previously. The data to be presented below are the results of an unavoidably subjective question on the regional quality of MLH 354 labour. The answers recorded are the subjective perceptions of respondents on the areas where MLH 354 labour would be most easily obtained. Nevertheless, these personal impressions are important, since, for many small and medium sized plants, detailed locational analysis in terms of location is never undertaken, and subjective impressions are acted upon as if they were fact.

An initial question enquired if the interviewee believed that his plant's labour supply and quality would be improved by a move to another region. A minority of 40 executives stated that they believed that their plant's location, with respect to labour supply and quality, would be improved by relocation. However, the larger proportion of North Western executives who thought a relocation would improve their labour supply is clear. (Table 8.11). These 40 executives were then asked to state, in their view, the most attractive region from a labour viewpoint. Table 8.12 presents the reactions to this enquiry. The most striking result to emerge from this table is the strong preference expressed by both North Western and South Eastern executives for the South East planning region (57.9 per cent and 47.6 per cent of survey plants respectively).

Certainly from the impression gained during interviews, the preponderance of North Western plants in Table 8.11 whose directors considered the South East to be the most attractive region for MLH 354 employment appeared to be based on the fact that the bulk of instrument industry workers are located in this region.

Table 8.11
Respondents believing that their labour supply and quality
would be improved by a move to another region

	North West		South East		Total	
	N	%	N	%	N	%
Would be improved	19	52.8	21	31.8	40	39.2
Would not be improved	17	47.2	45	68.2	62	60.8

N = 102

Table 8.12
Perceived best region for MLH 354 production

Standard planning region	North West		South East		Total	
	N	%	N	%	N	%
Scotland	-	-	1	4.8	1	2.5
Northern	-	-	1	4.8	1	2.5
North West	4	21.0	3	14.3	7	17.5
Yorks & Humberside	-	-	1	4.8	1	2.5
Wales & Mon	-	-	1	4.8	1	2.5
East Midlands	1	5.3	-	-	1	2.5
West Midlands	2	10.5	1	4.8	3	7.5
East Anglia	-	-	1	4.8	1	2.5
South East	11	57.9	10	47.6	21	52.5
South West	1	5.3	2	9.5	3	7.5

N = 40

However, in view of the complaints expressed by many South East
executives on the intense problems encountered when attempting to
obtain labour, this tendency in the North West for executives to
be attracted to the South East would appear to be based on false
assumptions. Misconceptions regarding MLH 354 labour supply in
the South East stems from a belief that a high concentration of
MLH 354 production is synonymous with a large and employable pool
of labour. Certainly in the instruments industry, and possibly
many other industrial categories, the labour pool concept is
false if it is meant to be defined as a reservoir of labour available
for employment. There are many MLH 354 employees in the South East
planning region because there are many MLH 354 establishments in
which they are employed.

There is generally no surplus of MLH 354 labour in the South East.
Firms established in the South East, or small firms of this region
in the process of growth, require labour in small numbers over a
protracted time scale. In such circumstances, the wide range of
skills available within the region may indeed be an advantage for
these South East firms. However, for an establishment wishing to
enter the South East from the North West or elsewhere, the task

of attracting a suitable number of skilled workers from the highly competitive South East labour environment would be difficult. Wage levels, rents, rates and the cost of private housing in the South East would present a considerable financial shock to such a firm. It will be evident from Table 8.12 that certain respondents in both the North West and South East planning regions interpreted the question on a move to another region below the planning region scale. In particular, several South Eastern establishments favoured a move to another region, but within the comparatively large South East planning region.

In most cases labour is obtained in the South East by attracting (or poaching) labour away from competitors. Poaching is necessary because virtually all MLH 354 labour is employed within existing companies. To poach labour requires the payment of above average wage levels, which may offset the advantages of such labour being locally 'poachable'. Firms in the South East have generally grown with these problems and have accepted them as part of their environment. However, plants entering the South East from the North West or elsewhere would experience a considerable shock, both in terms of obtaining suitable labour and its costs. Indeed, a move from the North West to the South East might be a case of 'out of the frying pan into the fire'.

8.11. THE PLANT'S EXISTING LABOUR FORCE: THE SINGLE MOST IMPORTANT LOCATION FACTOR

Before presenting the following data, it is important to understand the context of the question which provided the information. This question was not included in the labour section of the questionnaire, but was the final question of the survey questionnaire. It was separated from the labour section by four other major locational topics, and hence, labour considerations should not have been in the respondent's mind when the question was put. This final question enquired 'What is the single most important location factor affecting your business (i.e. the factor most crucial to the continued success of your plant)?'. Of the large range of factors which might have been selected, the significant number of 55 (53.9 per cent) respondents supplied answers which could be summarised as 'It is essential for the plant to remain in the present location since the loss of key personnel that would result from a relocation would put the business in serious jeopardy'.

This result further confirms the impression that MLH 354 firms are strongly oriented to existing workers. These workers possess the specialised knowledge of the firm and are the instrument's firm's most important asset. Such workers are frequently obtained over a period of years and, as a result, cumulatively increase the restraining influence of the labour force upon a firm in an existing location.

The single most important factor question produced a wide range of responses, but the 55 establishments considered above provided by far the largest group. Indeed, the second largest category of respondents consisted of a mere 9 plants. Thus, the status of the group of plants claiming labour constraints as the single most important factor is further enhanced. Moreover, these data are firmly supported by the observations made in the chapter on relocation which is concerned with the small number of plants which had relocated. The existing labour force is indeed a powerful restraining influence on the locational mobility of MLH 354 plants.

8.12. CONCLUSIONS

It has been shown in the introductory section of this chapter that the major concern of the location literature produced on labour has been directed at the effect of the spatial variability of labour factors on the location of mobile plants. Low emphasis has been generally placed upon the plant which is not mobile due to labour constraints which force the firm to reject a relocation solution to other organisational difficulties (e.g. lack of space).

The empirical work of this section has shown the instruments industry to be dominated by skilled and semi-skilled workers, with a high proportion of indirect employees. The perceptual data on the spatial variability of labour supply and quality has demonstrated that the enthusiasm shown by North Western respondents for the South East is unfounded and is based on the misconception that an area of high MLH 354 production may be equated with an available supply of suitable labour. It has been asserted that the impression of the availability of labour is as much created by the level of competition for such workers as by the absolute numbers of a labour force in any given area. The applicability of this factor, and other high costs, would appear to objectively render the South East planning region unattractive to firms which have not developed in this competitive environment.

The data gained from the final question of the interview survey suggests the strong general locational constraint imposed by the labour force on MLH 354 plants. Unprompted, and with a totally free choice, 55 respondents asserted that the constraint of labour was the most important locational factor affecting their plant. Since most MLH 354 establishments never undergo relocation the existing labour force of a plant grows with the establishment over a period of years. For high technology firms, and especially those of MLH 354, considerations of labour and location are dominated by the need to maintain the existing labour force and this, in turn, eliminates relocation over any long distance as possible company strategy. Relocation is considered, in the main, only after irresitible external pressure (e.g. redevelopment of site), and then, as will become evident from the chapter on relocation, over as short a distance as possible.

9 Behaviour

9.1. INTRODUCTION

Within the past fifteen years a considerable body of literature on
behaviour has emerged, in industrial geography and in other
academic disciplines (e.g. sociology, psychology and economics).
The most frequently studied topic, for industrial geographers,
has been the location decision making process (Luttrell 1962,
Greenhut and Colberg 1962, Townroe 1971, Cooper 1973). Much of
the methodological rationale for these studies derived from the
earlier work of researchers in the USA. Between the end of the
Second World War and the mid 1960's the contributions made by
Simon (1947,1955,1958,1959) and Cyert and March (1962) formed a
basis for much of the later work produced by industrial
geographers. Simon established the concept of 'boundedly rational
man' in the place of omniscient 'economic man'. Cyert and March
carried this proposition further, introducing a view of the firm
based on the notion that the organisational structure of an
enterprise consisted of a coalition of actors not always in
agreement with regard to policy.

However, the preoccupation of many researchers in industrial
geography with the location decision has meant that the bulk of
behavioural writing in industrial geography has been concerned with
mobile, or potentially mobile, sectors of industry. This
disproportional concern with location decision making has led
industrial geographers to largely ignore the locational implications
of the behaviour of executives operating within established firms
which are not mobile.

9.2. BEHAVIOUR AND MLH 354

The above comments are pertinent to MLH 354 because it became
clear that, in a study of an individual industrial sector, location
and re-location decisions are made by only a few directors of
manufacturing plants. Within a given time period only a minority
of firms relocate. This is particularly true for MLH 354 where,
of the 102 plants sample, only 15 plants had relocated within the
five years prior to the time of interview, and moreover, all of
these relocations were within the local area (i.e. from within a
30 mile radius of the present plant, see Chapter 10 on relocation).
Consequently, consideration of location decision making behaviour
is generally not relevant here since, in the majority of cases,
the location decision making process is curtailed by the decision
not to relocate.

However, although relocation rarely occurs within MLH 354,
behavioural factors may exert a location influence on the different

ways in which established MLH 354 establishments interact with and interpret their local business environment. Moreover, the plant's local environment contains evidence of the visible and objective results of such subjective attitudes. These physical realities may act as objective measures of the extent to which subjective behaviour of executives shape the individual plant's operational environment. Executive behaviour determines the degree to which individual plants are meshed into their local industrial milieu, causing varying degrees of locational inertia.

In conducting the investigation of such issues questions were included that sought to explore both the attitudes which cause functional realities and the objective ramifications of such behavioural attitudes. To this end, questions were devised which both sought to throw light on subjective evaluations and obtain objective facts. The analysis begins with a discussion of the replies to questions which attempted to observe respondents' evaluations of two subjective factors, the importance of local personal business contacts to location, and the perceived significance of amenity to the location of MLH 354 plants. These analyses will be followed by a detailed observation of the objective ramifications of subjective behavioural attitudes by observing the extent to which MLH 354 establishments obtain senior executive staff from the local area.

9.3. THE IMPORTANCE OF LOCAL PERSONAL BUSINESS CONTACTS

It has been previously asserted that an important component of material flow transactions is the personal bond that is developed between customer and vendor. Gilmour (1974) has noted that firm executives rarely examine all possible sources of material supply or bother to seek out the cheapest price for inputs. Bayliss and Edwards (1970) have further observed that the cheapest form of transport is rarely used by firms. An important factor that inhibits executives from seeking new or cheaper business relationships is the strong personal link that frequently evolves between themselves and their suppliers.

Because a known and trusted individual can be contacted within the supplying firm, problems can be dealt with quickly. Further, evaluations on the quality of service offered by a frequently used supplier are based on experience rather than estimates. Townroe (1971) believes that for certain industrial enterprises, local supply relationships may be important. He states, 'The answers given indicate that local suppliers are of importance in explaining the inertia of mobile or would be mobile concerns' (1971,p80). For many types of production a proportion of the inertia involved in these interactions may be a result of efficient personal contacts between customer and vendor.

The strength of local personal (face to face) contacts was tested for MLH 354. Interviewees were asked to evaluate local business contacts as being important, moderately important or unimportant. In Table 9.1 the strength of local business contacts is expressed against size of plant as it was considered likely that small plants would be more locally oriented in their business

contact patterns (as was asserted in the linkages section with regard
to material supply). The result of a chi square test performed on
Table 9.1 indicates a relatively weak level of significance at the
p = 0.01 per cent level. This result is of interest in that it
supports the results of the chi square test of the linkage section
(Importance of local supply relationships against size - Table 7.3),
in which a poor significance level of p = 0.02 per cent was achieved.
It would seem logical to conclude that where local supply
relationships are unimportant business contacts will be similarly
weak. Further, size of plant in both instances (Tables 7.3 and
9.1) does not seem to act as a determinant of firm linkage or
personal business contact patterns. In both Tables 7.3 and 9.1
a significant number of small plants considered local supply
relationships and personal contacts to be unimportant, in both
cases reducing the significance level of the chi square test.

Table 9.1
Importance of local business contacts against
size of plant

Plant size (number of employees)	Important		Moderately important		Unimportant	
	N	%*	N	%*	N	%*
1-19	5	55.6	3	33.3	1	11.1
20-49	13	41.9	9	29.1	9	29.0
50-99	9	40.9	5	22.7	8	36.4
100-199	1	8.3	4	33.3	7	58.4
200-499	3	18.7	5	31.3	8	50.0
500-999	1	11.1	5	55.6	3	33.3
1000+over	-	-	1	33.3	2	66.7

N = 102

Chi square 8.51   Significant at the p = 0.10 per cent level
* Proportion of total respondents in any given plant size category

It would appear reasonable to assert, as has been argued in the
linkages chapter of this study, that the weakness of local business
contacts reflects the dispersed input and output linkage patterns of
the instruments industry.

9.4. PERSONAL LOCATION AND AMENITY

Gibson (1970) suggested that the location of the instruments industry
in the USA was strongly influenced by the desire of technical and
managerial workers for amenity, either in the form of a peaceful
natural environment or of the cultural and entertainment attractions
of a large metropolis. Buswell and Lewis (1970) supported this
assertion in their study of the location of research establishments
in the United Kingdom. These findings are relevant since there is
an obvious link between the instruments industry and research
establishments in that both activities employ large numbers of
highly skilled technical and administrative staff. Both Gibson
and Buswell and Lewis argued that senior executive staff were
influenced in their personal location decisions by general
environmental quality.

Having ascertained that the long distance movement of MLH 354
plants was not in evidence, it was decided to test sample plants to
ascertain individual executive's appraisal of the attractiveness of
their known local environment with regard to the employment of highly
skilled technical and administrative personnel. An interesting
comparison may be made between the two study regions of the survey.
The North West includes areas of industrial dereliction and decline,
while the South East is largely associated with newer, cleaner
industry, and further boasts the cultural asset of the capital city
of London. Hence regional differences might be expected.

A general question enquired if respondents believed that there was
a strong preference among highly skilled technical and administrative
personnel for high amenity areas. Little difference in response
patterns was visible between the North West and South East planning
regions and in total 86 (84.3 per cent) of interviewees replied
affirmatively. However a further question was put to plant executives
in establishments which had been located at their current sites for
more than five years, asking if they considered their locations
attractive from an amenity viewpoint, in enhancing and promoting
the employment of highly skilled technical and administrative
personnel. The results of this question indicated that marginally
more plants in the South East (51.5 per cent of the South East total)
considered their location satisfactory compared with 44.4 per cent
of plants in the North West.

The respondents who considered their plants to be poorly located
from an amenity viewpoint were further asked if they considered the
problem to be critical, moderately important or unimportant. Of
the 41 respondents who considered their location unattractive, two
thought this problem critical, 23 thought it moderately important and
16 thought it unimportant (Table 9.2). The two plant executives
in the South East planning region who considered their amenity
problems to be critical might be viewed as anomalous since one
establishment was located in Teddington while the other plant was
situated in Southend on Sea. However, for the 'moderately important'
and 'unimportant' categories, the South East does appear to be
considered marginally more attractive than the North West.

Table 9.2
Locations considered unattractive from an amenity viewpoint:
extent of problem

Extent of problem	North West N	%	South East N	%	Total N	%
Critical	-	-	2	9.1	2	4.9
Moderately important	11	57.9	12	54.5	23	56.1
Unimportant	8	42.1	8	36.4	16	39.0

N = 41

An interesting note may be added here. During interviews in the
North West many interviewees working in poor environmental areas
forcefully made the point that environment and amenity were not
serious problems for higher income personnel since it was possible

to live up to 25 miles away from the plants in which they worked in attractive home environments. It is probably true that any area enclosed by a 25 mile circle centred on any plant in Britain would include at least one area of high amenity suitable for the residence of highly skilled technical and administrative staff. Since these people are most mobile, and are frequently the personnel who are asked to move with a re-locating plant, the poor environmental conditions that surround a factory are not as significant an influence as would be the case if the technical and administrative personnel were forced to live in its immediate environs.

The general impression gained from the questions on amenity and the employment of highly skilled technical and administrative personnel indicates that some consideration is probably given to the general quality of the environment when individual highly skilled technical and administrative staff move from job to job. However, the effect of such preferences on the ability of plants in poor amenity areas to attract highly skilled technical and managerial staff must be slight since although a significant number of plant executives interviewed considered that their location was not attractive from an amenity viewpoint, only two cases, in the South East, considered the problem critical. The difference between the North West and South East planning regions were visible but not as marked as might have been expected.

9.5. THE EMPLOYMENT OF LOCAL SENIOR EXECUTIVE STAFF

Before this analysis begins, the method by which the data were obtained must be explained. In order to obtain a general measure of the extent to which MLH 354 senior executives were of local origins a three part question was put to respondents. The question asked the origin of the plant's three most senior executives before joining (or establishing) the considered plant. If the origin (i.e. place of residence when previously employed or self-employed) was within a 30 miles radius of the considered plant, the individual was considered local. A simple scoring system was adopted in which the score given to the three most senior executives descended in direct relationship to their importance:

1st in importance	3 points
2nd in importance	2 points
3rd in importance	1 point

Thus a plant with all three of its most senior staff originating in the local area would score the maximum of six points. This would indicate not merely that the managing director was from the local area but that his second and third in command were also local men. The following first phase of the analysis attempts to isolate factors which bias the behaviour of MLH 354 plants in favour of the employment of local senior executive staff.

It has already been suggested that certain structural characteristics may influence the propensity of establishments to behave in a manner which favours the local industrial environment. Hill (1954) has noted that small firms are restricted in their operational environment and are frequently owned by local entrepreneurs. In order to test

Table 9.3

Local director's scores against size of plant

Scores

Size of plant (number of employees)	0		1		2		3		4		5		6	
	N	%*	N	%*	N	%*	N	%*	N	%*	N	%*	N	%*
1-19	-	-	-	-	-	-	-	-	-	-	-	-	9	100.0
20-49	6	19.4	-	-	-	-	1	3.2	4	12.9	1	3.2	19	61.3
50-99	1	4.6	2	9.1	-	-	5	22.7	-	-	-	-	14	63.6
100-199	2	16.7	-	-	2	16.7	4	33.3	-	-	-	-	4	33.3
200-499	5	31.2	1	6.3	-	-	3	18.7	1	6.3	-	-	6	37.5
500-999	6	66.7	-	-	-	-	1	11.1	-	-	-	-	2	22.2
1000+over	-	-	-	-	1	33.3	1	33.3	-	-	-	-	1	33.3
Totals	20	19.6	3	2.9	3	2.9	15	14.7	5	4.9	1	0.9	55	53.9

Chi square = 15.83   Significant at the p = 0.001 per cent level

* Proportion of total respondents' scores in any plant size category

N = 102

the assertions that small plant size, single plant status and local ownership were predominant determinants of local orientation, a series of chi square tests were performed on the scores recorded by sample plants in response to the question on the local origin of senior executive staff. These tests follow.

Local senior executives score and plant size

Table 4.5 of Chapter 4 has clearly shown that the small plant sub-sample is mainly comprised of independent firms. Such small businesses, through the restriction of limited resources, and more importantly through reliance upon their local environment, might be expected to be more locally oriented in the recruitment of senior executive staff. Further, since small plants are more likely to be locally owned (to be tested below) it might often be the case that the owner would have local acquaintances with known abilities who might be asked to join the business without recourse to advertising.

Table 9.3 plots plant scores for locally derived executives against size of plant. The chi square test performed on this table yielded strong significance at the $p = 0.001$ per cent level. Thus it may be accepted, from both a visual analysis of this table and from the highly significant chi square test, that there is indeed a greater propensity for small plants to employ local senior executives when compared with their larger MLH 354 counterparts.

Local senior executive score and single plant/multi plant status

Since it has been previously shown (Table 4.5) that small plants are predominantly single site independent firms, it might be expected that the test of this sub-section would reflect and support the test on local executive score and size of plant performed above. Further, it would appear logical to assume that a firm with a single location would be more spatially constrained

Table 9.4
Local directors' scores against multi/single plant dichotomy

Score	Single plant N	Single plant %*	Multi plant N	Multi plant %*	Total N	Total %*
0	6	30.0	14	70.0	20	19.6
1	-	-	3	100.0	3	2.9
2	1	33.3	2	66.7	3	2.9
3	2	13.3	13	86.7	15	14.7
4	2	40.0	3	60.0	5	4.9
5	-	-	1	100.0	1	0.9
6	36	65.5	19	34.5	55	53.9

$N = 102$

Chi square $= 16.78$ Significant at the $p = 0.001$ per cent level
* Proportion of total respondents in any given score category.

in its operations than an enterprise with two or more manufacturing sites from which it could potentially obtain materials and information

95

useful to the firm. Indeed, Table 9.4 confirms that plants
scoring highly for the employment of local senior executives are
predominantly single site independent firms. The chi square test
performed was strongly significant at the p = 0.001 per cent level.

Local senior executives score and locally owned businesses

Having established two major characteristics of plants utilising
local senior executives, it was decided to perform one further test
to establish whether local ownership might be a further determinant
of local senior executive employment. Table 9.5 indicates that
this third characteristic is indeed also strongly related to high
scores for the employment of local senior executives. Again the
chi score test recorded strong significance at the p = 0.001 per cent
level.

Table 9.5

Local ownership (within 30 mile radius) against local executives' score

Score	Locally owned		Other		Total	
	N	%*	N	%*	N	%*
0	5	25.0	15	75.0	20	19.6
1	1	33.3	2	66.7	3	2.9
2	1	33.3	2	66.7	3	2.9
3	3	20.0	12	80.0	15	14.7
4	2	40.0	3	60.0	5	4.9
5	1	100.0	-	-	1	0.9
6	41	74.5	14	25.5	55	53.9

N = 102

Chi square 15.50   Significant at the p = 0.001 per cent level
* Proportion of total respondents in any given score catefory

Hence, it may be deduced that the three characteristics of small
plant size, single plant status and local ownership are all strongly
related to plants scoring highly for the employment of locally
derived senior executive staff. These results may be taken to
indicate that generally a small scale of operation produces a
constraining influence on the operational environments of MLH 354
establishments. This assertion is further supported by the general
statistic which indicates that, of the 55 plants within the 102
plants main sample which scored the full six points for local origin
of senior executive staff, 36 (65.5 per cent) were locally owned
single plant firms employing less than 100 workers.

9.6. SPLINTERING AND MLH 354

However, the above analysis, although giving useful indications
of the general structural characteristics of the sample establishments
which make maximum use of local senior executive staff, does not
expose any spatial variations in the distribution of establishments
displaying these attributes. It has been proved that small firms
are more spatially restricted in their individual patterns of

senior executive staff employment. Further, it has been suggested
that this local organisation among small firms may result from a
rich network of local behavioural contacts. Hence, any spatial
clustering of small firms boasting maximum points scores for local
senior executive employment might be taken as an indication of
areas particularly suitable for the birth of MLH 354 enterprises.
Concentrations of small locally owned businesses employing local
senior executives might further indicate a form of splintering
whereby skilled personnel begin new businesses after working for
a large local MLH 354 producer. Evidence from the USA supports
this concept. Spiegelman (1964) has noted, 'The historical process
furthers clustering because new firms in the instruments industry
are typically formed by professionals who generally locate their
firms in the areas in which they are working' (p85). Thus these
new entrepreneurs gain advantages from a locally concentrated
MLH 354 skill environment.

In order to observe any concentrations of this type, the 38 smaller
firms which were locally owned, scored maximum points for the
employment of local executives, and employed less than 100 workers,
were plotted on maps of the North West and South East planning regions
in order to detect any clusters. (Clusters were defined by isolating
firms which formed a continuous group, with no individual plant of
the group detached from another by more than five miles).

In the North West planning region small clusters of plants are
identifiable in the Liverpool and Oldham areas while, in the South
East two small clusters are in evidence in the Windsor and Welwyn
Garden City areas, with larger clusters visible in the Wembley,
Park Royal area of North London, and in the Kingston, Merton,
Croydon area of South London (see triangles enclosed by faint
dotted lines, Figures 9.1 and 9.2). These areas are of particular
interest in that both the Liverpool and Oldham districts and
the Wembley, Park Royal and Kingston, Merton, Croydon districts
have been shown to be areas of intense MLH 354 employment (see
Chapter 8).

However, only limited success can be claimed for the above
spatial analysis in its role of identifying splintering effects
within areas of rich MLH 354 production. While four of the areas
noted above are indeed contained within areas of rich MLH 354
employment (see Figures 8.2 and 8.4), a large proportion of the
small locally owned firms scoring maximum points for local senior
executive employment in Figures 9.1 and 9.2 are relatively
isolated.

This limited success achieved by an attempt to indicate
splintering within a favourable MLH 354 environment may possibly
have been caused by the weakened applicability of the splintering
concept in a modern British context. The concept of splintering
may perhaps be best applied to the Victorian and Edwardian eras
when transport was relatively poor and expensive, and consequently
most employees lived near to the place of work. In such circumstances
an employee wishing to begin a new business would most probably do
so in the immediate vicinity of his previous employment. Thus,
splintering would be visible in the areas where the skills were
obtained.

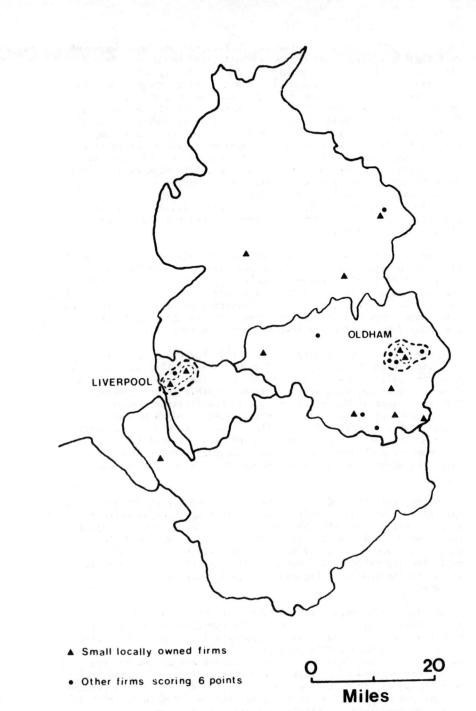

LIVERPOOL

OLDHAM

▲ Small locally owned firms

• Other firms scoring 6 points

0   20

Miles

Figure 9.1 Maximum points scoring establishments in the North West

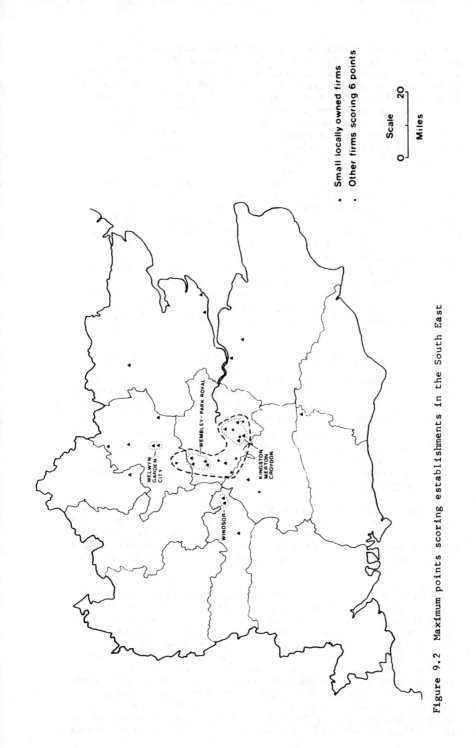

Small locally owned firms

. Other firms scoring 6 points

Scale

0 _____ 20

Miles

Figure 9.2 Maximum points scoring establishments in the South East

But in modern conditions of good transport and generally high personal mobility it is unrealistic to imagine that all new entrepreneurs will necessarily establish themselves in the immediate vicinity of their previous work places. Most workers in urban areas today (e.g. London and Manchester) travel considerable distances to work. Thus, a new entrepreneur may decide to begin a new business in his suburban home location, away from the firm and district in which his skills were obtained. Certainly, premises and rate costs would probably be lower in a suburban location when compared with the areas of high MLH 354 employment revealed in Figures 8.2 and 8.4.

The conclusion must be that even firms in isolated locations probably represent splintering from some source of MLH 354 expertise, but in a much more dispersed manner and over much further distances than has been catered for by the analysis of this sub-section. Rather than the analogy of seed bed growth, the parallel for a proportion of these small, relatively isolated, firms might be 'seeds cast to the wind'. This analogy would represent the migration of small firms to eccentric locations in which, due to their low executive and manual labour requirements, they are able to survive. However, it has been noted in the relocation section to follow that such firms may encounter serious problems stemming from the paucity of local skilled labour should expansion be envisaged.

9.7. THE ISOLATION OF RICH MLH 354 MANAGERIAL SKILL ENVIRONMENTS

The data on local senior executive employment scores is now adapted to a second phase of analysis. It is asserted that the existence of concentrations of plants possessing locally derived senior executives within a region denotes two major spatial characteristics:

1. A rich executive skill environment in which MLH 354 knowledge and expertise will be highly concentrated
2. The presence of a concentration of this senior executive labour will act as an indication of generally high levels of all types of MLH 354 labour.

Further, since areas of rich MLH 354 executive skill concentration are available to any MLH 354 firm, regardless of size or organisational status, all establishments scoring maximum points for the employment of local senior executives will be included in the following analysis. (These additional plants are represented by dots in Figures 9.1 and 9.2).

The addition of maximum points scoring plants which were not small single plant independent firms, produced an interesting strengthening effect on the local districts previously outlined in the above analysis of small locally owned firms (Triangles, Figures 9.1 and 9.2). In the North West, one further plant is added to the pair of plants forming the Liverpool district, while the Oldham cluster is increased from two to six plants (see areas enclosed by bold dotted lines). In the South East the addition of these extra plants forms a continuous crescent of maximum points scoring establishments which merges the Wembley, Park Royal district in the north of London with the Kingston, Merton, Croydon district in the south of the conurbation. The determinant of inclusion or exclusion

for these additional plants in these enlarged areas within the North
West and South East was the same five mile continuous grouping method
explained above. These enlarged areas are clearly indicative of
a degree of concentration of MLH 354 management expertise. The
individual district's share of maximum points scoring plants was
compared with the region's remaining maximum points scoring
plants and then set against the district and regional share of
total sample plants. These districts are dealt with in turn
below.

The Liverpool district

The relatively small group of four study sample plants in the
Liverpool district were analysed to detect any spatial bias
among establishments scoring maximum points for local senior
executives in favour of this area. Table 9.6 indicates a slight
2.5 per cent bias in favour of this district above the 11.1 per cent
figure which would have occurred had the maximum points scoring
sub-sample reflected the total sample distribution. Table 9.6
further indicates that, of the total number of four plants in
the district, three establishments scored maximum points for
the employment of local senior executive staff. However, the
small size of the Liverpool group of maximum points scoring
establishments precluded any significant results in this area.

Table 9.6

Proportion of local executive maximum points scoring plants in the
Liverpool district compared with the total sample distribution

	District		Rest of planning region		Region Total	
	N	%	N	%	N	%
Maximum points scoring plants	3	13.6	19	86.4	22	100.0
All sample plants	4	11.1	32	88.9	36	100.0

The Oldham district

The Oldham district contained the major concentration of maximum
points scoring plants in the North West. Table 9.7 again
compares the extent to which the maximum points scoring plants of
the Oldham district represent a spatial bias within the total
sub-sample of maximum points scoring establishments in the
North West region. A significant spatial bias of 7.8 per cent
was indicated above the 19.4 per cent which would have been
recorded had the distribution of local executive plants spatially
reflected the total study sample. Moreover, table 9.7 also
provides strong proof of the dominance of the maximum points
scoring establishments within the Oldham district since of the
seven study sample plants within this district, six scored
maximum points for local senior executive staff.

Table 9.7

Proportion of local executive maximum points scoring plants in the
Oldham district compared with the total sample distribution

	District		Rest of planning region		Region Total	
	N	%	N	%	N	%
Maximum points scoring plants	6	27.3	16	72.7	22	100.0
All sample plants	7	19.4	29	80.6	36	100.0

The Wembley, Park Royal - Kingston, Merton, Croydon 'crescent' district

This area, predominantly confined within Greater London, is the
largest of the three districts considered here, in both area and
numbers of plants. Table 9.8 indicates that a 10.6 per cent bias
in favour of the district exists above the 37.9 per cent which would
have been expected had the maximum points scoring plants' sub-sample
reflected the total study sample distribution. This is the largest
bias of all the districts considered. As in the above instances,
Table 9.8 clearly indicates that 16 (64 per cent) of the main sample
plants in this district scored maximum points, again confirming the
dominance of maximum points scoring plants over all sample
establishments within the areas isolated in Figures 9.1 and 9.2.

Table 9.8

Proportion of local executive maximum points scoring plants in the
Wembley, Park Royal - Kingston, Merton,
Croydon 'crescent' district compared
with the total sample distribution

	District		Rest of planning region		Region Total	
	N	%	N	%	N	%
Maximum points scoring plants	16	48.5	17	51.5	33	100.0
All sample plants	25	37.9	41	62.1	66	100.0

9.8. THE DISTRIBUTION OF LARGE AND NON-LOCALLY OWNED ESTABLISHMENTS IN THE 'CRESCENT'

After plotting together all the maximum points scoring plants in
Figure 9.2, it was noted that although, as previously recorded,
the small locally owned plants were generally scattered throughout
the South East planning region, the other establishments scoring
maximum points (ie. plants not locally owned and/or employing
over 100 workers) appeared, on cursory visual examination, to be
highly concentrated in the crescent.

Table 9.9

A comparison of the distribution of large/non-locally owned maximum points scoring plants in the 'crescent' with total distribution

	'Crescent' (other)						Rest of South East (other)						Regional total (other)					
	Small locally owned plants		Large non-locally owned plants		Total		Small locally owned plants		Large non-locally owned plants		Total		Small locally owned plants		Large non-locally owned plants		Total	
	N	%	N	%	N	%	N	%	N	%	N	%	N	%	N	%	N	%
Maximum points scoring plants	9	36.0	7	87.5	16	48.5	16	64.0	1	12.5	17	51.5	25	100.0	8	100.0	33	100.0
All sample plants	12	37.5	13	39.4	25	37.9	21	65.6	20	60.6	41	62.1	33	100.0	33	100.0	66	100.0

To pursue this interesting observation further the maximum points scoring plants displayed in the crescent in Table 9.8 were divided into 'small locally owned' and 'other' categories and tabulated in Table 9.9. A small minority of establishments in this 'other' category employed less than 100 workers but were not locally owned. However, for the purpose of the present analysis they were included with the large plants since their owners, who employed executive staff, were all large conglomerate companies with employment behaviour more in tune with large plants than the small locally owned group of businesses. As in Table 9.8 the method of comparing the distribution of a sub-sample against the distribution of the total sample and observing any percentage difference is again used here.

The results of this further analysis are most striking. Of the eight large and/or non-locally owned maximum points scoring plants in the South East planning region, seven establishments were included in the crescent. These seven plants when expressed as a percentage of all 'other' plants scoring maximum points represented 87.5 per cent of this category in the South East. Moreover, this figure of 87.5 per cent was 48.1 per cent higher than would have been the case had these 'other' maximum points scoring plants mirrored the South Eastern distribution of all sample plants (Table 9.9).

In many ways these large concentrations of 'other' plants scoring maximum points in the crescent might be expected. It is reasonable to generally assume that the senior executives of larger and non-locally controlled plants are more likely to be professional managers than actual owners of the plants at which they work, as is frequently the case among small locally owned firms. Large plants, in which shareholders are the owners, employ professional managers to fill executive positions. Hence, it should be of no surprise if concentrations of MLH 354 managerial expertise available in local labour markets should be more extensively utilised by such large and non-locally controlled plants.

In the above context these large and/or non-locally controlled establishments may be viewed as more effective delimiters of MLH 354 managerial skill environments, since such predominantly large organisations both create, and are attracted to, areas where a variety of specialist MLH 354 skills are available. Conversely, the executive requirements of a small independent firm may frequently be provided by the owner, whose home location is in the local area of the company. It has been previously noted that small locally owned firms are not strikingly concentrated in the urban crescent. The weaker orientation of such establishments to both executive and skilled manual MLH 354 labour must result in part from the lower demands created by a small workforce and an internalised system of executive employment based on personal local business contacts which are not dependent on the local MLH 354 job market quality.

9.9 CONCLUSIONS

The aspatial tests on the size structure and ownership characteristics

of plants scoring maximum points for local senior executive employment
indicated that small plant size, single plant status and local
ownership were all predominant features among plants scoring maximum
points for the employment of local senior staff.

The analysis of the data on the origin of senior executive staff
has produced further significant results. Weakest here was the
material ensuing from an attempt to isolate splintering effects
whereby small locally owned firms might be detectable in clusters
which, in turn, would indicate areas highly suitable for the birth
of MLH 354 firms. Certain small clusters were observed which were
later supported by further analysis which indicated that these
areas were indeed strong concentrations of instrument industry
activity.

The further analysis performed on the local senior executive
score data, including all plants scoring maximum points for local
senior executive staff, regardless of size or organisational status,
proved beneficial in isolating districts of important MLH 354
executive skill concentrations. The analysis of large and/or
non-locally owned maximum points scoring plants has produced
interesting detailed evidence of a greater propensity for this
category of establishment to be strongly oriented to rich urban
MLH 354 managerial skill environments in the South East.

However, in such circumstances, the expert labour of these
districts can be viewed as a constraining influence on the location
of MLH 354 production, rather than an attraction to instrument
industry manufacturers. The distinction between constraint and
attraction is important, since for many other locational
considerations (e.g. cost of building, rates and congestion),
the district clusters in Figures 9.1 and 9.2 are generally in
unsatisfactory areas. But the importance of labour orientation
overrides these lesser disadvantages, and MLH 354 plants remain in
otherwise poor locations because of the need to orientate towards
skilled labour.

Most probably this is why the initial subjective questions on
the importance of local personal business contacts and amenity
produced inconclusive results. Compared with labour considerations,
such factors are largely insignificant. Behavioural factors may
have more influence on mobile firms in generally footloose
industries where location choices hinge on small differences,
subjectively interpreted. However, within MLH 354, where labour
orientation is the dominant location consideration, the unavoidable
importance of this single factor tends to pre-empt consideration of
other location criteria which are clearly of lesser importance.

10 New location and relocation

10.1. INTRODUCTION

The study of the factors which determine the location of mobile industrial plants has received much attention during the post war period (Katona and Morgan 1952, Hague and Newman 1952, Luttrell 1962, Cameron and Clark 1966, Townroe 1971, Northcott 1977). Both Luttrell and Townroe have attributed the growth of industrial mobility and the subsequent post-war increase in industrial location studies to governmental distribution of industry policies. Luttrell (1962) has noted that, until 1939, a need for increased manufacturing space could be met by a simple in situ expansion. But this option has been severely curtailed since the war by the introduction of Industrial Development Certificates in those parts of the South East and West Midlands experiencing growth.

Hence, firms which require an IDC for any substantial expansion have been frequently forced to consider a medium or long distance expansion in place of the pre-war solution of growth on site. For firms undertaking long distance relocation, a choice may exist between a complete relocation and the opening of a branch plant. Faced with this choice, many firms have opted for the establishment of a branch, since as Townroe (1971) has noted, the opening of a branch factory has the great advantage of gaining the required increase in capacity without disrupting existing production levels.

However, the results of many empirical studies have shown that mobile firms will initially seek to restrict their movement distance to a minimum. Mobile firms will first search the local area for either a larger factory to accommodate a complete relocation or for smaller premises in which to establish a branch plant. It is no surprise that the local area should appeal to relocating firms. By retaining operations within the local area material and information linkages, transport arrangements, and the labour force may be maintained in the new location. Firms are especially keen to retain their skilled key workers and a local relocation avoids asking employees to move. Thus, the resistance among firms towards government attempts, through IDC's, to enforce long distance moves is generally strong and has been observed frequently (Loasby 1966, Townroe 1971).

It is important to stress, however, that the relocation of production is not a frequent phenomenon. Townroe (1971, p35) has noted that 'For the vast majority of companies the question of finding a new location for a manufacturing plant rarely, if ever, arises'. Moreover, it has been frequently observed by researchers in regional development that the number of mobile firms is closely tied to the general economic performance of the nation. Many of the studies of mobile industry since 1945 have analysed establishments across a wide range of technology (Greenhut and Colberg 1962, Cameron and Clark 1965, Townroe 1971, Northcott 1977). One reason for this multi sectoral approach to mobile industry has been the frequent lack of a viable number of mobile plants in any single industrial category during a viable time period.

10.2. LOCATION AND MLH 354

The above discussion is relevant to MLH 354 in that only fifteen relocations and three new plants were identified within the present study sample, within a period of five years prior to the survey date. Further, all the relocations were within the local area (ie. the previous plant was within 30 miles of the current location). Hence, many considerations of critical importance to firms moving long distances did not apply to these MLH 354 relocations since many functional relationships had remained unchanged. It had been assumed that there would be at least a small minority of establishments within the 102 plant sample which had relocated over a distance greater than 30 miles. Consequently, interview questions were devised to assess the effect of changes in the complete range of functional relationships important to firms relocating over long distances. But clearly, the relocation questions set in a national context were inapplicable.

Remembering the considerations in the introduction above, the total absence of long distance moves in MLH 354 is not surprising. Three reasons may be proposed as explanations of why MLH 354 plants have not been forced into long distance moves by the government. First, MLH 354 plants are frequently small and, on account of low space requirements, do not seek buildings in excess of the government's 12,000 sq.ft. IDC expansion threshold when relocating. Second, the majority of MLH 354 production is 'clean' in that it does not present environmental problems and, as a result, is more acceptable to local planning departments. And third, MLH 354 plants have a good case to argue for not relocating over long distances since a large proportion of their skilled labour force would not relocate with them.

10.3. NEW LOCATION AND RELOCATION IN THE MAIN SURVEY SAMPLE

The extent to which relocation was anticipated by executives in established MLH 354 plants

In advance of the analysis of new and relocated plants, a single general question was put to executives of established plants. The question enquired if plans were in progress towards relocation, or if it had been considered but rejected, or finally if it had never been considered. Table 10.1 indicates that 78.6 per cent of the sub-sample respondents replied that relocation had never been considered. Of the remaining eighteen plants, eleven had considered relocation but had rejected a move, while seven establishments were in the process of moving.

107

Table 10.1
Consideration of relocation

Relocation decision	North West N	%	South East N	%	Total N	%
Considered but rejected	1	3.3	10	18.5	11	13.1
Had never been considered	29	96.7	37	68.5	66	78.6
In progress towards relocation	-	-	7	13.0	7	8.3

N = 84

However, it is significant to note that ten of the eleven plants which had considered relocation, and all of the plants in the process of moving, were from the South East planning region. The predominance of South Eastern plants in these two categories of Table 10.1 may reflect the greater prosperity of South East businesses, since prosperity may lead to expansion and the subsequent need for more production floorspace. Moreover, the South East propensity for considering movement must also be influenced by more stringent planning controls in force in the South East and their more rigid application. In view of the earlier comments on branch plants, it should be noted that it is easier for North West plants in need of new capacity to purchase a branch factory in their local area. This negates the need for expanding businesses to relocate the existing plant. The availability in the North West of suitable empty mill buildings of attractive size and cost, combined with weaker planning controls, provides the North West industrialist with greater flexibility than his South East counterpart.

Conversely, the South East entrepreneur is under constant pressure through planning legislation and redevelopment schemes which either restrict development or force movement through the compulsory purchase of the existing plant. This assertion is supported by the existence of five inner London plants in the seven plant sub-sample which were in the process of relocation. There can be little doubt that increased costs resulting from higher rates and rents, and incresed transport congestion, in conjunction with strong centrifugal government planning pressures towards peripheral areas of Britain, have greatly contributed to the increased tendency for South Eastern businesses to analyse their locations with a view to possible moves.

Causes of relocation

Consideration is now given to the fifteen plants which relocated during the five year period prior to the survey date. Of these fifteen plants, ten were relocations (15.2 per cent of the South East total) in the South East, while five (13.9 per cent of the North West total) were in the North West. Table 10.2 indicates the reasons given by plant executives for their relocation.

The causes of the relocations are surprisingly few, and may be summarised as reorganisation, more space needed, lost site to re-development and lease ran out, rent increased, decided to move. Interestingly these reasons have been observed in other research (Townroe 1971). Again in support of the results of Table 10.1, where the South East planning region accounted for all the imminent plant relocations, the two plants in Table 10.2 which had lost their sites to redevelopment were also from the South East planning region. Moreover, the higher number of South East responses to the 'more space needed' alternative reflects the arguments proposed on prosperity and planning controls, which relate to plants in the South East.

Table 10.2
Reasons for relocation

	North West		South East		Total	
	N	%	N	%	N	%
Reorganisation	2	40.0	-	-	2	13.3
More space needed	2	40.0	7	70.0	9	60.0
Lost site to redevelopment	-	-	2	20.0	2	13.3
Lease expired new rent too high	1	20.0	1	10.0	2	13.3

N = 15

10.4. ATTITUDES TOWARDS GOVERNMENT INCENTIVES

The fifteen relocated and three new plants were asked a question to ascertain their behaviour towards government incentives. In analysing Table 10.3 it should be remembered that no relocations involved movement from the planning region of the original location. This explains much of the information in this table. Clearly, it explains why no South Eastern firm took up grants and incentives, there being no incentives of offer in the South East. Conversely, the existence of government aided plants in the North West planning region reflects the existence of assisted areas.

Table 10.3
Government grants and incentives

	North West		South East		Total	
	N	%	N	%	N	%
Considered	2	33.3	6	50.0	8	44.4
Taken up	2	33.3	-	-	2	11.1
Not considered	2	33.3	6	50.0	8	44.4

N = 18

Most surprisingly, eight of the eighteen (44.4 per cent) answering plants did not consider government assistance at all. Although strong reasons have been given in Chapter 8 on Labour, for the necessity of short distance moves, the lack of any consideration of government incentives that might attracts plants further afield indicates, for these eight plants, an extremely restricted sphere of information pertaining to the location decision. The fault may lie with poor Department of Industry publicity.

However, a strong resistance by certain executives towards any government involvement in the location decision was apparent. Townroe (1973, p47) has noted, 'The British system of planning controls and regional incentives also introduces the uncertainties (as seen by many industrial managers) of contact with officialdom'. Although too much should not be claimed of the results from an eighteen plant sub-sample, this data on government incentives and their take-up suggests that liaison between the Department of Industry and relocating firms could be improved.

10.5. LABOUR ORIENTATION AND LOCATION

An initial question enquired of the three new and fifteen relocated plants if regional differences in wage levels had influenced the location decision. This produced only one affirmative reply. This response would be expected if it is considered that orientation to an existing skilled labour force was the paramount location consideration. A subsequent question enquired if the Regional Employment Premium had been considered during the location decision process. While four plant executives had considered the REP, none of these companies subsequently took up this incentive.

The failure of mobile MLH 354 plants to take advantage of the REP can be readily understood as the incentive is most attractive to establishments that employ large numbers of unskilled workers. Indeed both Luttrell (1962) and Townroe (1971) have observed that certain firms are encouraged to relocate by the need to orientate in favour of large supplies of unskilled and semi-skilled labour. Clearly for such firms REP presents a welcome incentive. However, for MLH 354 firms, any advantage gained by the REP incentive would be more than dissipated by the loss in productivity that would ensue from the need to replace key personnel not moving with the plant concerned. Replacements for key workers within MLH 354 are especially difficult to train due to the high technology nature of the industry, and this has been noted empirically (see Case Study C of this Chapter).

A final question enquiring if the location choice of the three new and fifteen relocated plants was influenced by a desire to orient in favour of a particularly good localised supply of labour bore convincing results. Originally the question had been designed to accommodate both long and short distance relocations but, since long distance moves were absent, questions on long distance relocation did not apply. However, the plants which did relocate locally almost unanimously acknowledged that orientation to skilled labour strongly influenced their decision.

Table 10.4 indicates that, of the fifteen relocating plants,
thirteen indicated that their location decisions had been influenced
by a desire to orient in favour of existing local workers. Hence
these results, taken in conjunction with the findings of the
chapter on Labour, confirm that MLH 354 location and relocation is
dominated by the need to retain existing workers. Table 10.2
has indicated that relocation, when it occurs, is predominantly
forced upon MLH 354 establishments and is only reluctantly
undertaken. In these circumstances, the best strategy adopted by
MLH 354 businesses which are forced to relocate is to move over
the shortest distance possible in order that the existing
workforce might be retained.

Table 10.4
Orientation to a supply of local labour

	North West		South East		Total	
	N	%	N	%	N	%
Skilled	2	40.0	2	20.0	4	26.7
Highly skilled tech/managerial	-	-	1	10.0	1	6.7
All types	1	20.0	7	70.0	8	53.3
Not relevant	2	40.0	-	-	2	13.3

N = 15

10.6. LONG DISTANCE MOVES WITHIN THE INSTRUMENTS INDUSTRY

Analysis has shown that MLH 354 plants are severly constrained to
existing locations by their labour forces. It has been argued that
the dearth of long distance relocations within the industry results
directly from the unwillingness of plants to risk the loss of
valued skilled members of the workforce. Hence, it was considered
of importance to this hypothesis to obtain a limited number of
MLH 354 case study plants which had undertaken long distance
relocations. By interviewing the directors of such establishments
the validity of these assertions could be tested.

However, such was the scarcity of these moves that the general
survey restrictions of movement within the past five years and
relocation to one of the two main study planning regions were
abandoned. Personal contacts made during the interview survey
were used, in conjunction with formal questionnaire data, to isolate
three companies which had undertaken long distance relocations.
Two of the establishments contacted were originally disqualified
from the relocation classification becuase they relocated more
than five years before the survey date. The final plant was obtained
through consultation with a senior executive of a multi plant
organisation who provided information on a relocation which was
not included in the main survey sample of this study, since the
plant had relocated to Cornwall.

The three plants which argeed to provide material for case
study analysis had no objections to their names being used in

111

this study. The establishments examined are given below with their relocation dates:

A: Wilmot Breeden Electronics Ltd.   1964
B: Shandon Southern Products Ltd.   1971
C: Teddington Autocontrols Ltd.   1968

The establishments were contacted by means of a specially designed postal questionnaire. The most important features of the data obtined are summarised here.

A: Wilmot Breeden Electronics Ltd.

Wilmot Breeden Electronics, formerly the Wayne Kerr Company, moved from Kingston Upon Thames to Bognor Regis in 1964. The firm manufactures electronic measuring equipment and now employs 187 workers. Problems that might have arisen as a result of the lengthy interval since relocation were minimised by the fact that the managing director interviewed remembered, and was centrally involved in, the relocation process.

The main objective of this particular relocation was to consolidate, under one roof, production and research and development that had previously been performed in two separate plants. Land rents and labour costs were also considered to be lower on the South Coast. Strong pressure from the Department of Industry for a development area move was firmly resisted. It was felt that the chosen medium range move of approximately 48 miles would be more acceptable to the key personnel required to move with the firm. The seaside location was considered a further attraction for key workers.

The general appraisal of the importance of linkages and transport orientation in the new location appeared to indicate a decline in efficiency in the new South Coast location. Such decreases in convenience were considered moderately inconvenient but not critical. However, as might be expected, problems resulting from the supply of labour in the new location were evident. As indicated in Table 10.5, little difficulty was experienced in attracting managerial staff to the new location. In this instance the relocation distance was small,

Table 10.5
Wilmot Breeden Electronics Ltd. - Long distance movement of personnel

	Top Admin. and Tech.		Foreman/ Supervisor		Shop Floor	
	Male	Female	Male	Female	Male	Female
Asked to move	3	-	2	-	65	-
Did move	3	-	2	-	15	-
Acquired after move*	-	-	-	-	100	-

* During first year of operation only

key managerial staff were few in number and the new location was attractive. Further, the loyalty of executive staff is more frequently assured by the wish to maintain positions that might not be achievable in other organisations, especially for older members of the company's staff. Firms may, moreover, feel able to offer promotion or financial inducements to this minority which would not be feasible if offered to all employees.

Conversely, Table 10.5 also indicates that only fifteen of the 65 shop floor employees who were asked to move with the firm actually transferred to Bognor Regis. These skilled and semi-skilled workers included lathe and milling machine operators, groups of workers in constant short supply, who clearly decided, in the majority of instances, to remain in the Kingston upon Thames area and obtain employment with another company. Since such workers are frequently housed in council property, any advantage to these shop floor workers in making a personal relocation are much reduced in comparison with their managerial counterparts.

When asked to state the main advantage gained through relocation, the managing director asserted firmly that increased efficiency had been achieved by the concentration of the firm's activities on one site. However, the biggest disadvantage of the new location was a shortage of skilled and semi-skilled shop floor workers, resulting both from a poor rate of removal of these employees during re-location (Table 10.5) and from the shortage of suitable workers in the Bognor Regis area. It should be remembered that the problem of the scarcity of skilled labour is exacerbated for MLH 354 plants because frequently they do not merely require skilled labour that would meet the needs of a generaly engineering firm. The lathe and milling machine operators required by instrument firms are the most accomplished members of these skill groups.

B: Shandon Southern Products Ltd.

Shandon Southern Products Ltd. is a company now employing 154 workers and is engaged in the manufacture of analytical instruments. Consolidation was again the main force towards relocation. A manufacturing facility at Camberley (Surrey), possessing 20 per cent of the organisation's total manufacturing output and all the company's administration and research and development facilities, was closed in 1971, and these activities were moved to an existing production plant at Runcorn. The Runcorn plant had been in operation since 1968 on a new government built factory estate and had previously manufactured 80 per cent of the company's production, but possessed little administration.

Having decided to concentrate production on one site, the decision remained as to which site to close and, more important, which group of workers should be asked to move. It was decided to close the Camberley site and to move its activities to Runcorn for two main reasons. First, with its smaller 20 per cent of production, disruption of output would be less. Second, considerable government assistance was available at the Runcorn location. At the time of interview the plant had obtained, or was receiving, capital grants of 22 per cent on the cost of all equipment, Regional Employment Premium and Temporary Employment Subsidy.

Changes in linkage and transport patterns due to the relocation were considered unimportant. This was a result of the major production location remaining unchanged. However, this case study is worthy of particular note because of the generally high skill levels of the workforce required to move. Further, the environmental contrast between Camberley and Runcorn is physically sharp, and might have been expected to act as a deterrant to staff asked to move to the North West. In contrast to the situation in case study A, a considerable number of highly skilled technical and managerial staff were being asked to move, thus compounding the problem. Indeed, Table 10.6 indicates that, of the 13 highly skilled technical and aministrative staff asked to move, a mere five accepted.

Table 10.6
Shandon Southern Products Ltd. - Long distance movement of personnel

	Top Admin. and Tech.		Foreman/ Supervisor		Shop Floor	
	Male	Female	Male	Female	Male	Female
Asked to move	13	-	-	-	-	-
Did move	5	-	-	-	-	-
Acquired after move*	14	2	-	-	8	2

*During first year of operation only

As with establishment A, the major advantage claimed from the relocation was the consolidation of all the firm's activities under one roof. But the price paid for this improvement was high. It may be noted from Table 10.6 that certain highly skilled technical and administrative personnel refused to make the move to Runcorn, creating problems with organisation and efficiency. Further, a 'shortage of local scientific engineering and skilled manpower' (questionnaire extract) that had been present since the Runcorn plant's initial establishment in 1968, intensified after the Camberley relocation. At the time of interview, this problem had virtually forced the parent company to close the Runcorn plant. Only after the company had managed to persuade the government that the plant was certain to close, was Temporary Employment Subsidy extended to the Runcorn establishment on the basis that workers were continuing in employment who would otherwise have become unemployed. The problems resulting from an environment devoid of MLH 354 skills would appear to be a critical location problem for mobile plants.

C: Teddington Autocontrols Ltd.

The relocation of Teddington Autocontrols involved a move from within the South East planning region at Sunbury on Thames to St. Austell in Cornwall. The company, a multi-plant organisation, manufacturing a wide range of MLH 354 products, indicated two major reasons for their relocation.

First, the original site at Sunbury on Thames was located only a few hundred yards from an access point to the new M3 motorway. A part of the site which originally accommodated 1,800 employees was sold at a considerable profit for the building of a depot for a firm distributing consumer goods. The capital gain obtained was the major reason for the relocation, which was necessitated by the subsequently reduced site area. Second, the company considered that competition from other firms in the Sunbury on Thames area (notably those associated with London Airport) was causing labour costs to be unacceptably high. The new St. Austell location was expected to be a cheaper employment area.

St. Austell was chosen as the location for the new plant partly because an establishment belonging to the group was already in operation, and material linkages were planned between the plant at Camborne and the new St. Austell factory. The establishment of the St. Austell plant resulted in the Sunbury on Thames factory's workforce being reduced to 219 employees, while 830 workers were transferred to, or employed at, the new St. Austell location. Surprisingly, the decision was also taken to move the company's headquarters to St. Austell. Government incentives were acknowledged as a further major reason for the selection of the St. Austell site. Grants received included Regional Employment Premium, capital grants on all new equipment of up to 20 per cent, transfer grants for all key workers and a grant towards the building costs of the St. Austell factory.

The peripheral national location of St. Austell might have been expected to present general communication problems. Indeed, unlike plants A and B, the respondent for Teddington Autocontrols acknowledged moderate inconvenience in the obtaining of material inputs and the distribution of outputs. A critical decline in the general level of convenience of functional linkage flows both in material and information, was noted. These communication problems were a direct result of the division of the company's major activities between the Sunbury and St. Austell plants. The problem centred on the need for semi-finished items of production to pass between the two plants. Transport problems resulting from poor road conditions were further noted as exacerbating the material flow problems. Moreover, it was asserted that the quality of material suppliers in the local St. Austell area was inferior to that in the Sunbury on Thames area.

As might be anticipated with a change in the location of the headquarters, the majority of workers who were asked to move over this long distance were in the highly skilled technical and managerial category. Table 10.7 indicates that moderate success was achieved

Table 10.7
Teddington Autocontrols Ltd. - Long distance movement of personnel

	Top Admin. and Tech.		Foreman/ Supervisor		Shop Floor	
	Male	Female	Male	Female	Male	Female
Asked to move	63	2	10	-	10	1
Did move	45	1	4	-	7	1
Acquired after move*	120	40	6	14	100	600

*During first year of operation only

throughout the employee skill type categories. However, 18 of the
63 technical and managerial members of staff who were asked to move
refused to leave the London area. Table 10.7 also shows that the
aim of employing a large number of semi-skilled predominantly
female staff from the local area had been achieved.

The interviewee, in this case the senior personnel manager of the
company, made special comment on the personal problems that the
new location had created. Criticism was made of the 'lack of
intellectual, artistic and cultural entertainments and lack of
high class shopping and civic amenities' (questionnaire response).
It is indeed ironic that, for some individuals, the advantages of
an attractive physical environment are out weighed by the lack of
cultural amenities that are obtainable in a physically poor urban
environment. Certainly for those accustomed to the cultural
advantages of an urban existence, the movement to Cornwall might
cause severe problems of social adjustment and, more important,
the prospect might deter workers from migrating this long distance.

The major advantage gained from the new location was attested to
be a 'cheaper and more stable labour force' (questionnaire extract).
However, the main disadvantage was described as 'a period of
sustained production and supply difficulties which resulted from
inadequate training and knowledge of new staff, which so badly
affected sales, it was exceptionally difficult to recover'
(questionnaire extract). In this case, as in case studies A and
B, the disruption to production caused by the loss through
movement, and the scarcity after movement, of skilled and semi-
skilled MLH 354 labour, has caused major problems.

10.7. CONCLUSIONS

It must be re-affirmed that relocation is not a frequent phenomenon
in MLH 354. However, through analysis of the plants derived from
the main sample which had recently either newly located or relocated
over short distances, and of the three long distance relocation
case study establishments, a deeper perspective on the reasons why
the majority of MLH 354 establishments do not relocate has been
developed. It has been ascertained from established plants that
inertia, created by a highly valued and immobile local workforce,
has seriously constrained MLH 354 producers to their existing
locations. By analysing the small numbers of plants which have
undertaken relocation, these general assertions on the importance
of the labour force in the location decision process have been
tested and shown to be critical.

11 The location of MLH 354: a synthesis

11.1. INTRODUCTION

The conclusions to this study are presented in two parts. This
chapter contains interim conclusions on the empirical chapters of
the research (Chapters three to ten). The first aim will be to
establish the general themes which have been established as important
by the results of the field survey. After isolating the factors
which influence the general location of MLH 354 production, Chapter 12
will move into a final phase of analysis which will discuss these
factors in the light of existing theoretical writings on location
theory and high technology industry.

A fundamental influence on all the location factors isolated in
the fieldwork has been the consistently high technology nature of
MLH 354 production. However, not all the effects of MLH 354
technology viewed in the context of these various location factors
have been of locational significance. For example, the high value
added nature of MLH 354 output and the consequently low proportion
of transport costs as a percentage of total costs, had tended to
render transport considerations of low locational significance to
MLH 354 production. Conversely, the over-riding importance of high
quality labour has been critical to the location of MLH 354 plants.
The importance of labour derives directly from the particular high
technology and labour intensive production methods inherent in
instrument industry manufacture. Hence, in a general sense, the
extent to which any of the location factors examined in this study
are considered relevant to the distribution of MLH 354 production
result from the effects of production technology.

Thus the following summary will be constructed on the premise that
the location factors considered in the empirical sections of this
work may be divided into significant and insignificant location
influencing groups. Further in all these cases the summary will
indicate the manner in which MLH 354 high technology production has
shaped the relevance of industrial location factors. To this end,
the following synthesis will be divided into two parts. First the
major locational factors considered to be of insignificant
importance to MLH 354 location will be analysed. This will be
followed by a consideration of labour, the significant location
influencing factor.

11.2. FACTORS INSIGNIFICANT TO THE LOCATION OF MLH 354 PRODUCTION

Organisation

The enquiries undertaken to establish the organisational characteristics of MLH 354 were not expected to yield factors of great locational significance. However, it was anticipated that some form of locational effect might result from the activity of multi site companies in MLH 354. Work produced by several researchers (Luttrell 1962, Cameron and Clark 1966, Parsons 1972, Townroe 1971), has suggested that the control of company headquarters on subsidiary branches can be strong in many sectors. Such control frequently affects the location of such plants in a manner more conversant with company group strategy than with any general locational criteria (Oakey, 1979).

However, in the case of MLH 354, a powerfully consistent pattern of independence emerged from the multi-plant establishments within the survey sample of this study. On a wide range of considerations covering freedom to purchase, research and development, executive control and staffing levels, a high degree of autonomy was detected at plant level. Further, this independence from other group plants was evidenced in the organisation of linkage contacts in respect of both markets and materials.

The major reason for this high degree of plant level independence was the high technology nature of MLH 354 production methods. Such specialised forms of production offer little opportunity for large scale linkage flows with other group plants, since the output of individual MLH 354 plants is generally both diverse in type and complex in specification. Hence, decision making in branch plants within multi site MLH 354 companies is frequently left to individual executives at plant level who are best qualified to assess organisational problems and adopt optimal strategies. This phenomenon largely results from the technical sophistication of MLH 354 production.

Moreover, it was noted that takeover and merger activity within MLH 354 was dominated by firms external to the instruments industry. Because these frequently large companies were predominantly external to MLH 354, they tended to purchase going concerns. The purchasing of a factory with all administrative and techncial personnel intact negated the need for specialised MLH 354 expertise. It was suggested that the lack of acquisition activity from within MLH 354 was due to poor profits within the instruments industry which stem from an inability to standardise production and introduce mass production methods. While a wide range of products may offer the security of diversified markets, such a strategy strongly inhibits the introduction of mass production methods which might produce economies of scale. In this connection, it should be remembered that according to figures given in Chapter 3 (on structure), small plants achieved a greater output per head than their larger counterparts. Indeed, the inability of large MLH 354 establishments to standardise production constantly reoccurred as an important factor in other analytical chapters.

Hence, both the independence of MLH 354 establishments and the low level of take over activity in survey sample plants may be largely explained by the high technology nature of instrument industry production. The analysis of organisation in this study has indicated that the points discussed above do strongly influence the organisational structure of MLH 354 plants. However, they have been

118

included in the locationally insignificant factors grouping for the purpose of this summary because these characteristics do not have any significant locational effect. Indeed, the great autonomy indicated by the branch plant sub-sample suggests that spatial distortions produced by any form of group behaviour is largely absent in the MLH 354 context.

Information

When factors of potential importance to MLH 354 location were being taken into consideration for analysis, information was readily isolated as a topic of great possible relevance to the location of MLH 354 production. Work from the USA (Deuterman 1966, Gibson 1970) suggested that important technical information contacts might exist between instrument industry firms and research establishments. However, the present analysis of the importance of technical information to the British instruments industry (Chapter 5), although it proved to be interesting, largely eliminated the concept of locationally important ties between MLH 354 plants and research establishments.

It was discovered that an important reason for the low use of external research establishments in Britain, when compared with the USA, was the lack of contract research facilities. It was observed that universities and other research establishments were used for gaining low level library information. However, the critical innovative technical information needed for the development of new products was predominantly obtained from internal research performed in the factory. A critical distinction was made between information which is available and may be accessed in approximate proportion to the amount of search initiated, and other innovative information concerning the new product designs which is highly confidential in nature.

Again, the highly specialised high technology nature of MLH 354 production may be indicated as a strong influence on the information acquisition behaviour of MLH 354 plants. In an industry where product specification can be frequently more important than price, new innovations are constantly sought after and, when obtained, are closely guarded. This has led British instrument industry establishments, in the absence of any formalised external contract research facilities, to internalise important research activities. Consequently, the locational effects of information gathering are rendered of slight importance.

Transport

Transport was found to be of low locational importance to MLH 354 production since the costs of transport are a very low proportion of total costs in this high value added industry. This is certainly true if compared with the powerful influence of labour on the location of MLH 354 plants. However, important characteristics of interest were isolated by the analysis of transport (Chapter 6). In particular, transport quality emerged as an important consideration for MLH 354 plants.

Speed, safe handling and security were all shown to be aspects of quality of importance to MLH 354 plants. Further, in an industry where value of output is consistently high, and exports are important, air transport and the proximate location of an airport were shown to be of enhanced value. However, while not locationally critical, the significance of these transport factors can be clearly attributed to the nature of instrument industry production. Due to the generally high value of MLH 354 products, most methods of transporting goods to customers are conomically viable for instrument industry firms. Further, the high value of these goods demands that the risk of damage or loss should be minimised during transit. Hence, MLH 354 plants are more concerned with safe arrival than price when modes of transport are considered. But, in general terms, it was considered that these quality considerations do not have any strong impact on the location of MLH 354 production.

Linkages

Many of the above remarks on transport may also be applied to linkages insofar as they affect the location of MLH 354 production. Both inputs to, and certainly outputs from, MLH 354 plants are of consistently high value. Hence, it was not expected that orientation to any market or material source would be evidenced by MLH 354 plants. The analysis presented in Chapter 7 shows conclusively that, save in the case of certain forms of sub-contracting, both backward and forward local linkages are generally unimportant to MLH 354 plants. The strength of these findings was enhanced by a further analysis of multi plant establishments and their intra group local linkage patterns. Again, as with the general sample results on linkages, local material linkages, for both the inputs and outputs of this multi plant sub-sample, were found to be extremely weak.

Yet again the high technology nature of MLH 354 production is central to an understanding of this weak linkage effect on the location of MLH 354 plants. Due to the complexity of individual products and to the diversity of product ranges, MLH 354 plants are unable to obtain inputs or maintain markets in their local area. Aided by the high value (and frequently low weight) of commodities which flow between MLH 354 plants and their customers and suppliers, spatially dispersed linkage patterns are economically possible. This is indeed fortunate, since forward and backward linkages are often necessary over long distances in order to satisfy highly precise needs.

Hence, the spatially diverse patterns of MLH 354 linkages and the highly specialised nature of requirements negate, in the majority of cases, the possibility of local market or supply linkage orientation. This reality, and the other considerations examined above, strongly indicate that the diverse nature of MLH 354 production technology has again produced a powerful effect on the importance of linkages to instrument industry production, which in this case was observed to be insignificant.

11.3. LABOUR, THE LOCATION FACTOR SIGNIFICANT TO THE LOCATION OF MLH 354 PRODUCTION

The importance of labour to MLH 354 has been made apparent throughout the three previous chapters. It is paradoxical to note that the same

technological factors (i.e. complex range of products, high technology)
which have rendered the factors considered above locationally
insignificant conversely provide much of the basis for the importance
of labour to MLH 354.

The high skill requirements of MLH 354 establishments necessitate
the acquiring not merely of skilled workers, but of the most highly
proficient operatives in any given skill group (e.g. lathe and
milling machine operators are a good example of this phenomenon).
The growth of the individual plant is characterised by the employment
of occasional additional workers over a protracted time period, and
with each new employee, the plant becomes more constrained to the
existing location. The general shortage of MLH 354 workers, even
in areas of high instrument industry production, ensures that a
long distance relocation undertaken by an individual establishment
from such an area will result in other local businessmen poaching
skilled labour from the mobile plant. Employees are less likely
to relocate with a plant if alternative employment exists locally.

The spatial concentrations of plants evident in the chapters on
labour and behaviour must predominantly result from the advantages
afforded by rich areas of MLH 354 expert labour. However, much of
the rationale for the continued existence of these concentrations
would appear to stem from the inertia inherent in the immobility of
the existing workforces of firms, rather than by any positive attraction of firms to these rich MLH 354 labour environments.

For, although MLH 354 skills are generally abundant in these
concentrations, any employment advantages which might be gained by
a plant in these areas is largely negated by the intense competition
from the many other local businesses. The poor environmental
condition of large parts of these areas from other locational
viewpoints (e.g. transport congestion, little space for expansion,
pollution) merely strengthens the proposition that such MLH 354
establishments are indeed the victims of intense labour inertia.

11.4. SIGNIFICANT AND INSIGNIFICANT LOCATION FACTORS: SOME
THEORETICAL COMMENTS

In order to aid the clarity of the following concepts Figure 11.1
has been constructed. All the factors considered under the above
significant and insignificant headings are included in the model,
but they are contrasted in a slightly different manner under either
a 'material' or 'human' resource factor heading. Initially,
Figure 11.1 may be viewed in a general industrial context.

This figure indicates human and material resource factors in terms
of varying degrees of internal plant level control. The locational
importance of any factor (e.g. raw materials, labour) will be
dependent upon the level of technology employed in the individual
plant. Each resource factor will possess an attracting force which
will be determined by its importance to the technology of the
individual plant. However, in this model organisation is removed
from this external and largely inflexible human and material
resource environment, since organisation is completely flexible in
the sense that it is determined internally, and is under the control

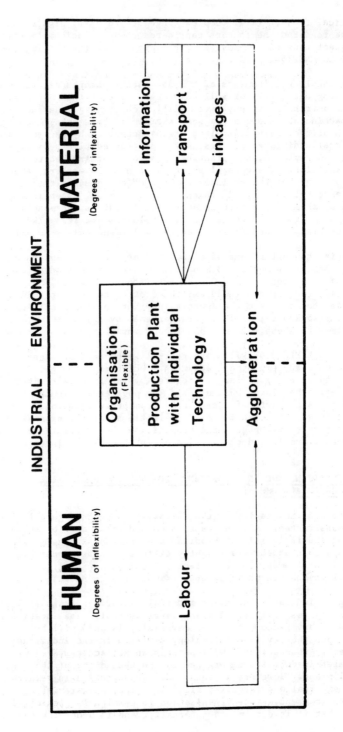

Figure 11.1 Model of human and material effects on plant location

of executives.

The material and human location influencing resource factors are indicated to possess degrees of inflexibility, implying that the importance of such resources will vary between industries, and where they are important, will restrict the location options of a given plant. For certain industries which are truly footloose, both sets of human and material factors migh be largely ignored; but for others, the neglect of one of these location influencing resources might mean reduced profits or even bankruptcy. Agglomeration effects are also included in the model and it is indicated that both material and labour resource factors contribute to any attraction of an agglomeration on the production plant.

Having established that the model in Figure 11.1 might be applied to any technological type of production at the conceptual level, the discussion now applies the results of the present survey data to the model. The significant and insignificant labels previously attached to the human (labour) and material (information, transport, linkages) groups of factors may now be safely re-applied, since these are assertions which stem directly from the results of this study.

The effects of material resources have generally been of insignificant locational importance to MLH 354 production plants. Earlier in this chapter, MLH 354 technology was indicated as a major reason for this lack of significance. Those who have claimed that instrument industry is footloose would appear to base their assertions on a partial consideration of purely material resource factors (Spiegelman 1964, Farness 1968).

Although it is accepted that a degree of variability might exist in the interpretation of the importance of material factors by plant executives, the factors themselves are more susceptible to objective assessment in that they can be expressed in terms of economic costs to the firm with some accuracy. However, the human characteristic established to be of critical importance to the location of MLH 354 plants is difficult to cost because the resource itself is subjective in nature. While it is generally possible to predict the potential cost of transport or material supplies in a new location, it is a daunting task to predict the cost of labour in a new location. Further, the rate at which new workers acquire skills in the new location may also be unpredictable. Much will depend on the number of key workers who can be persuaded to relocate with the mobile plant, which in turn depends on many factors which are not all financially based. Shop floor workers in particular tend to put greater emphasis on a known environment with the advantages of friends and relations. Gitlow's assertion (1954) on the labour force moving in direct response to differences in the spatial distribution of wage levels would appear simplistic in the face of the results of this study.

Traditional economic views of labour and its effect on the location of industry is another area for further theoretical consideration in the final chapter of this study. Certainly, the results indicating the importance of labour to MLH 354 show that the production of instruments cannot be considered to be footloose. The final chapter of this study relates the significant results of this research to relevant location

123

theory, and considers the implications of the findings for high technology industry. In keeping with the methodological rationale of this work no attempt will be made to claim universal relevance for these results to all high technology industry. Hence, the final conclusions will be restricted to those areas of theory to which useful contributions might be made.

12 Conclusions

12.1. LABOUR: THE CRITICAL LOCATION FACTOR

Severe qualifications must be made to certain generalisations on
the mobility of labour insofar as MLH 354 is concerned. In particular,
the views of Gitlow (1954) and Smith (1971) on the mobility of
labour need qualification. Smith (1971, p45) claims that 'If the
right kind of workers are not available at a location that is otherwise attractive, it may be possible to obtain them from other areas
or from other local employers, since labour is mobile both
geographically and in terms of occupation'. This study has shown
conclusively that such assertions are not a satisfactory general
explanation of the effects of labour on the location of instrument
plants.

Since many types of labour are largely immobile in the short term,
it follows that a proportion of firms must orientate to labour
instead of the reverse procedure invoked by Gitlow and Smith. Hence
in such circumstances, the spatial uniqueness and quality of the
required labour force will inhibit industrial firms to varying
degrees, depending on the nature of production. An establishment
requiring simple machine minding operatives could clearly locate in
any area of high unemployment, since the simplicity of the tasks
required to be performed could be accomplished by virtually any male
or female workers. However, a firm with MLH 354's skill requirements
would experience severe difficulties of establishment and continued
profitability in areas where suitable labour was not available;
the case studies in Chapter 10 lend weight to this view.

The problems of instrument industry relocation are confirmed by
Luttrell (1962) who detected a significant difference between the
establishment of two branch plants by a single instrument firm.
The first branch plant to be opened concentrated on unsophisticated
parts of the firm's production range. Consequently, labour was
easily obtained and a high level of success in the new location
was achieved. However, the second branch plant to be opened was
entrusted with a more sophisticated range of products which in
turn caused considerable difficulty in the obtaining of the necessary
skilled labour.

But even for firms with moderate skill requirements such as the
motor industry, labour problems may arise after relocation from the
lack of suitable local skilled labour (Goodman and Samuel 1966).
Hence, for all firms, the level of the spatial constraint presented
by labour will be determined by the nature of production adopted by
the individual firm. Further, in most cases, mobile industry must
move to labour, with the degree of constraint that this imposes
depending on the spatial distribution of the particular type of labour
required.

However, in the situation previously described in this study, and by Luttrell, where the constraint of labour on mobility may be severe, the effect of existing workers on established firms is a restraining influene. Riley (1973) noted that the distribution of the motor vehicle industry in its early stages of development was constrained by local skilled labour, a situation which was later radically altered by mass production methods. But significantly it has been a recurrent observation in the above analysis that the inability of MLH 354 plants to introduce labour saving process machinery has been an important characteristic in influencing the balance of resource inputs to present day instrument industry production. Thus, unlike the modern motor industry, MLH 354 remains locationally constrained by existing skilled labour to existing locations.

It is of further importance to assert the nature of the constraint of skilled labour ôn the location of MLH 354 production. Gibson (1970), in his study of the distribution of the instruments industry in the USA, was convinced that the location of instrument industry production was strongly influenced by the distribution of highly skilled technical and administrative professional personnel. However, his attempt to correlate the distribution of these highly qualified workers with instrument industry production was only moderately successful. He stressed the importance of professional workers at the expense of their shop floor counterparts because he considered that 'The striking feature of labour inputs in Instruments and Related Products is not the production workforce, but rather the great dependence on professionals e.g. scientists and engineers' (Gibson 1970, p357).

Although it is accepted that research and development personnel are important to instrument industry production, the effect of the distribution of highly skilled workers would not seem a strong influence on the location of the British instruments industry. Certainly, this study has indicated that such highly skilled workers are the most mobile of MLH 354 employees and hence the most likely to move to the job. Clearly such workers may gain increased financial benefits or enhanced status through a factory relocation. Conversely, skilled shop floor workers are relatively immobile. Not having undergone the breaking of local ties facilitated by a higher education in a distant locale, the shop floor worker maintains strong personal and family ties in his local area. Further, such workers are frequently housed in council housing which may not be available in new locations. The shop floor worker has little to gain and much to lose by a personal move.

In many firms in other industrial sectors, the refusal of shop floor workers to relocate with a mobile plant might result in such employees being replaced by workers obtained in the new location. However, in the MLH 354 example many such workers might be considered irreplaceable. Hence, it is more an orientation to the existing shop floor workers that has created the locational inertia within MLH 354 than a concern for higher skilled technical and administrative staff.

The above conclusions, when viewed in the context of existing literature indicate that insufficient detailed attention has been

paid to the variable effects of labour on the location of industrial
firms. This is not to assert that labour has not been considered,
but that the attention paid has in many instances been in over
generalised terms. Researchers have frequently ignored the effects
of technology by using multi sectoral survey samples and not
stressing the important part played by production technology in
determining the locational constraints imposed by labour (Townroe
1971, 1975, Northcott 1977). Moreover, labour is far too frequently
considered a resource factor, obtained in a similar manner to
material inputs to the production process. In this context, many
assertions on the mobility of labour can be viewed as absurd.
Labour is a resource which comprises of human beings, and hence
manifests the unique and important input characteristic of being
itself behavioural in nature. In such circumstances the laws of
supply and demand and movement to greater advantage cannot be
rigidly applied.

The works of Simon (1947,1955,1958,1959) and Cyert and March (1962)
would seem to be as applicable to the behaviour of those for whom
industrial location decisions are made (and their reactions) as
they are to the employers who make them. However, due to the preoccupation with the location decision making process within mobile
firms, the location decision making behaviour of executive personnel
has dominated behavioural studies within industrial geography.
Little concern seems apparent for the large numbers of industrial
firms which are constrained not by the immobility of materials but
rather by the mainly behaviourally derived immobility of essential
workers as in the MLH 354 instance.

It is accepted that MLH 354 is an example of an industry which is
exceptionally dominated by labour for the many reasons given in this
text. However, for the most mobile of firms, in the absence of
government restrictions, the existence of a known and valued workforce, including many individuals who would not relocate over long
distance, would be more than enough reason for dispelling any
ideas of relocation. However, it is probable that the generally
constraining effect of labour for all forms of industrial production
has been understated in recent writings within industrial geography.

12.2. IMPLICATIONS FOR HIGH TECHNOLOGY INDUSTRIES

This study has shown that a high technology industry is not necessarily
characterised by sophisticated production methods and mass markets.
It is clear from the MLH 354 example that the combined effects of
custom built products, fragmented markets, and rapid technological
obsolescence means that the scope for process machinery in production
is low and production costs remain high. Economic viability is
ensured by the high prices that MLH 354 products can command. However,
the inability of large plants to introduce economies of scale either
through purchasing or production process mechanisation was noted
at several stages in the study and was particularly evident in their
inferior output per head performance noted in Chapter 3.

While it is generally accepted that high technology industries are
dependent on highly skilled management and development personnel,
this study has shown that the less mobile skilled shop floor worker

is the major cause of MLH 354 labour orientation. Although the instruments industry might be an extreme case, the results on the importance of skilled shop floor labour must be to some extent applicable to many other high technology industries where a high level of mechanisation of production is not possible and skilled shop floor workers are required. Since training periods for highly skilled shop floor craftsmen are long, the short and medium term recruitment strategy of MLH 354 firms must be oriented towards trained skilled workers.

The shortage of experienced shop floor personnel causes expanding firms to be careful not to loose their existing workers, while attempting to poach additional workers from competitors. Thus an extremely intense job market exists in areas where MLH 354 production is concentrated. But this phenomenon has far wider implications for regional development. First, since the skills of MLH 354 production are of value to other high technology industries, there will be a strengthening of already existing areas of specialisation, mainly in the more prosperous South East. Indeed, since other high technology industries such as computers and electronics are also common in the South East, an area of broader high technology specialisation will be mutually reinforcing. Second, although high technology industries may be expanding, the skill structures of the development region labour markets are not attractive to firms seeking the skills applicable to high technology forms of production. The reluctance of the government sponsored INMOS enterprise to agree to a development area location for their first production plant highlights the problem for these areas. They are trapped in a vicious circle. Because they have few high technology industries they are unattractive to new high technology forms of production, and hence their industrial mix remains dominated by aging or unprofitable industries (e.g. iron and steel, shipbuilding).

The industrial sectors which expanded to create the mobile industry boom between 1950 and 1970 generally required a reasonable proportion of unskilled or semi-skilled workers, which without the need for retraining, alleviated unemployment in the development regions (e.g. motor vehicles, textiles). But any new high technology industries which could be tempted to development regions are unlikely to compensate for the continued decline in unskilled and semi-skilled employment in the development regions. Apart from the above observation that high technology industries are more strongly attracted to existing areas of specialisation, the proportion of unskilled jobs provided by such forms of production would be much lower than the industrial sectors that provided much development area employment in the past through mobile industry. While training and retraining are clearly possible solutions to particular skill shortages, the case study evidence from the present survey shows that considerable problems of production disruption can occur when training is attempted in high technology industries.

Although it would be inappropriate to claim that the results of this study are applicable to all high technology industries, the MLH 354 example has hinted that high technology industry may be far less locationally robust than previous areas of industrial growth in the

post war period. While the potential for wealth creation in high
technology industries might be great, there appears less likelihood
that such industries will act as a suitable vehicle for redressing
the imbalances caused by sectoral industrial decline, especially
in the development regions.

Bibliography

Alonso, W. 'The economics of urban size', Papers and Proceedings of the Regional Science Association, 26, pp 67-83, 1971

ASTMS, Technical change, employment and the need for collective bargaining, Discussion Paper, 1978

Barron, I. and Curnow, R. The future with microelectronics, Francis Pinter Ltd., London, 1979

Bayliss, B.T. and Edwards, S.L. Industrial demand for transport, H.M.S.O., 1970

Blackbourn, A. 'The spatial behaviour of American firms in Western Europe', Spatial perspectives on industrial organisation and decision making, Hamilton F.E.I. (Ed.), pp 245-264, Wiley, London, 1974

Buswell, R.J. and Lewis, E.W., 'The geographic distribution of industrial research activity', Regional Studies, 4,2, pp 297-306, 1970

Cameron, G.C. and Clark, B.D. 'Industrial movement and the regional problem', University of Glasgow Social and Economic Studies, Occasional Paper No.5, Oliver & Boyd, Glasgow, 1966

Chapman, K. 'Agglomeration and linkage in the U.K. petro-chemical industry', Trans., IBG, 60, pp 33-68, 1973

Clegg, H.A. 'The mobility of labour', National Provincial Bank Review, pp 9-13, May 1965

Cooper, M.J.M. 'The industrial location decision model', Unpublished Ph.D. Thesis, Univ. of Birmingham, 1973

Cotterill, C.H. Industrial plant location: its application to zinc smelting, American Zinc, Lead and Smelting Co., Saint Louis, 1950

Cyert, R.M. and March, J.G. A behavioural theory of the firm, Prentice Hall, Englewood Cliffs, N.J., 1963

Department of Industry Business Statistics Office, The directory of businesses: instrument engineering, electrical engineering, H.M.S.O., 164, 1968

Department of Industry Business Statistics Office, Business Monitor Quarterly Statistics, H.M.S.O., PQ 354, 1972,1973, 1974, 1975

Department of Industry Business Statistics Office, Business Monitor, Reports of the Census of Production, H.M.S.O., Part 63, 1963, C70,1968, 1970, PA 354, 1971, 1972

Deutermann, E.P. 'Seeding science based industry, New England Business Review, pp 7-15, December 1966

Dicken, P. 'Some aspects of the decision making behaviour of business organisations', Economic Geography, 47, pp 426-438, 1971

Edwards, S.L. 'Transport costs in British industry', Journal of Transport Economics and Policy, 4, pp 265-283, 1970

Farness, D.H. 'Identification of "footloose" industries', Annals of Regional Science, 2, pp 303-311, 1968

Fulton, M. and Hoch, L.C. 'Transport factors affecting location decisions', Economic Geography, 35, pp 51-59, 1959

Gibson, J.L. 'An analysis of the location of instrument manufacture in the United States', AAAG, 60, 2, pp 352-367, 1970

Gilmour, J.M. 'External economies of scale, inter-industrial linkages and decision making in manufacturing', Spatial perspectives on industrial organisation and decision making, Hamilton, F.E.I. (Ed.), pp 335-363, Wiley, London, 1974

Gitlow, A.L. 'Wages and the allocation of employment', Southern Economic Journal, 21, pp 62-83, 1954

Goddard, J.B. 'The location of non-manufacturing activities within manufacturing industries', Hamilton, F.E.I., (Ed.), Contemporary Industrialisation, pp 62-85, Longman, London, 1978

Goddard, J.B. and Smith, I. 'Changes in corporate control in the British urban system, 1972-77', Environment and Planning a,10, pp 1073-1084, 1978

Goodman, J.F.B. and Samuel, P.J. 'The motor industry in a development area: a case study of the labour factor', British Journal of Industrial Relations, 9, pp 335-365, 1966

Greenhut, M.L. and Colberg, M.R. Factors in the location of Florida industry, Florida State University, Tallahalasse, 1962

Hague, D.C. and Newman, P.K. Costs of alternative locations; the clothing industry, NIESR and Cambridge University Press, 1952

Hill, C. 'Some aspects of industrial location', Journal of Industrial Economics, 2, pp 184-192, 1954

Hines, C. and Searle, G. Automatic unemployment, Earth Resources Research Ltd., London, 1979

Hoare, A.G. 'International airports as growth poles: a case study of Heathrow airport', Trans., IBG, 63, pp 75-96, 1974

Hoover, E.M. Location theory and the shoe and leather industries, Harvard University Press, Cambridge, Mass., 1937

Karaska, G.T. 'Manufacturing linkages in the Philadelphia economy: some evidence of external agglomeration forces', Geographical Analysis, 1, 4, pp 354-369, 1969

Katona,G. and Morgan, J. 'The quantitative study of factors determining business decisions', Quarterly Journal of Economics, 66, pp 67-90, 1952

Keeble, D.E. 'Industrial decentralisation and the metropolis: the north west London case', Trans., IBG, 44, pp 1-54, 1968

Keeble, D.E. 'Local industrial linkage and manufacturing growth in outer London', Town Planning Review, 40, pp 163-188, 1969

Leigh, R. and North, D.J. 'Regional aspects of acquisition activity in British manufacturing industry', Regional Studies, 12, pp 227-245, 1978

Lever, W.F. 'Industrial movement, spatial association and functional linkages', Regional Studies, 6, pp 371-384, 1972

Lever, W.F. 'Manufacturing linkages and the search for suppliers and markets', Spatial perspectives on industrial organisation and decision making, Hamilton, F.E.I. (Ed.), pp 309-333, Wiley, London, 1974

Lloyd, P.E. and Dicken, P. Location in space: a theoretical approach to economic geography, Harper International, New York, 1972

Loasby, B.J. 'Making location policy work', Lloyds Bank Review, 83, pp 34-47, January, 1966

Lösch, A. The economics of location, Yale Univ. Press, New Haven, 1954

Luttrell, W.F. Factory location and industrial movement, NIESR, London, 1962

Mc Nee, R.B. 'A systems approach of understanding the geographic behaviour of organisations, especially large corporations', Spatial perspectives on industrial organisation and decision making, Hamilton F.E.I. (Ed.), pp 47-75, Wiley, London, 1974

Martin, J.E. Greater London: an industrial geography, Bell, London, 1966

Moseley, M.J. and Townroe, P.M. 'Linkage adjustment following industrial movement', TESG, 64. 3, pp 137-144, 1973

North, D.J. 'The process of locational change in different manufacturing organisations', Spatial perspectives on industrial organisation and decision making, Hamilton, F.E.I. (Ed.), pp 213-224, Wiley, London, 1974

Northcott, J. 'Industry in the development areas: the experience of new firms opening factories', Broadsheet 573, Political and Economic Planning (PEP), London, 1977

Oakey, R.P. ' Technological change and regional development; a note on policy implications', Area, 11, 4, pp 340-344, 1979

Parsons, G.F. 'The giant manufacturing corporations and balanced regional growth in Britain', Area, 4, 2, pp 99-103, 1972

Pred, A.R. 'The concentration of high value added manufacturing', Economic Geography, 41, pp 108-132, 1965

Pred, A.R. and Tornqvist, G. Systems of cities and information flows, 2 vols, Lund University, 1973

Rayner, D. Directory of United Kingdom Instrument Manufacturers, David Rayner Publications, Chelmsford, 1974

Rees, J. 'The industrial corporation and location decision analysis', Area, 4, pp 199-205, 1972

Rees, J. 'Decision making, the growth of the firm and the business environment', Spatial perspectives on industrial organisation and decision making, Hamilton F.E.I. (Ed), pp 169-211, Wiley, London, 1974

Riley, R.C. Industrial geography, Chatto and Windus, London, 1973

Simon, H.A. Administrative behaviour, Macmillan, London, 1947

Simon, H.A. 'A behavioural model of ration choice', Quarterly Journal of Economics, 69, pp 98-118, 1955

Simon, H.A. 'The role of expectation in an adaptive behaviouristic model', Experimentation, uncertainty and business behaviour, Bowman, J. (Ed.), SSRC, New York, 1958

Simon, H.A. 'Theories of decision making in economic and behavioural science', American Economic Review, 49, pp 253-383, 1959

Smith, D.M. 'A theoretical framework for industrial geographical studies in industrial location', Economic Geography, 42, pp 95-113, 1966

Smith, D.M. 'On throwing Weber out with the bathwater; a note on industrial location and linkage', Area, 1, pp 15-18, 1970

Smith, D.M. Industrial location, Wiley, New York, 1971

Smith, I.J. 'The effect of external takeovers on manufacturing employment change in the Northern Region between 1963 and 1973', Regional Studies, 13, pp 421-437, 1979

Speigelman, R.G. 'A method of analysing the location characteristics of footloose industries; a case study of the precision instruments industry', Land Economics, 40, pp 79-86, 1964

Stafford, H.A. 'The anatomy of the location decision: content analysis of case studies', Spatial perspectives on industrial organisation and decision making, Hamilton, F.E.I. (Ed.), pp169-188, Wiley, London, 1974

Taylor, M.J. Spatial linkage in the West Midlands' iron foundary industry, Unpublished Ph.D. thesis, University of London, 1971

Thorngren, B. 'How do contact patterns affect regional development', Environment and Planning, 2, pp 409-27, 1970

Townroe, P.M. 'Industrial location decisions', University of Birmingham Centre for Urban and Regional Studies, Occasional Paper, 15, 1971

Townroe, P.M. 'Industrial location search behaviour', Monographs in Geography, Rees, J. and Newby, P. (Eds.), Middlesex Polytechnic, 1, 1973

Vyver, F.T.de. 'labour factors in the industrial development of the South', Southern Economics Journal, 18, pp 189-205

Wallace, I. 'The relation between freight transport organisation and industrial linkage in Britain', Trans., IBG, 61, pp 25-43, 1974

Warren, K. 'Recent changes in the grographical location of the British Steel Industry', Geographical Journal, pp 343-361, 1969

Webber, M.J. 'Sub-optimal behaviour and the concept of maximum profit theory', Australian Geographical Studies, 7, pp 1-8, 1968

Weber, A. Alfred Weber's theory of the location of industry, Trans. Friedrich, C.J., University of Chicago Press, 1929

Wise, M.J. 'On the evolution of the gun and jewellery quarters in Birmingham', Trans., IBG, pp 57-72, 1949